DATE DUE

Herman Melville

THE PROFILES IN LITERATURE SERIES

GENERAL EDITOR: B. C. SOUTHAM, M.A., B.LITT. (OXON.)
*Formerly Department of English, Westfield College,
University of London*

Volumes in the series include

CHARLOTTE BRONTË	Arthur Pollard *University of Hull*
CHARLES DICKENS	Martin Fido, *University of Leeds*
HENRY FIELDING	C. J. Rawson, *University of Warwick*
JAMES JOYCE	Arnold Goldman, *University of Sussex*
THOMAS LOVE PEACOCK	Carl Dawson, *University of California*
SAMUEL RICHARDSON	A. M. Kearney, *Chorley College of Education*
WALTER SCOTT	Robin Mayhead, *University of Ghana*
JONATHAN SWIFT	Kathleen Williams, *University of California*
ZOLA	Philip Walker, *University of California*

Herman Melville

by D. E. S. Maxwell
Professor of English,
York University,
Toronto

LONDON
ROUTLEDGE & KEGAN PAUL
NEW YORK: HUMANITIES PRESS

First published 1968
by Routledge & Kegan Paul Ltd
Broadway House, 68–74 Carter Lane
London, E.C.4

Printed in Great Britain
by Northumberland Press Limited
Gateshead

SBN 7100 2955 1

The Profiles in Literature Series

This series is designed to provide the student of literature and the general reader with a brief and helpful introduction to the major novelists and prose writers in English, American and foreign literature.

Each volume will provide an account of an individual author's writing career and works, through a series of carefully chosen extracts illustrating the major aspects of the author's art. These extracts are accompanied by commentary and analysis, drawing attention to particular features of the style and treatment. There is no pretence, of course, that a study of extracts can give a sense of the works as a whole, but this selective approach enables the reader to focus his attention upon specific features, and to be informed in his approach by experienced critics and scholars who are contributing to the series.

The volumes will provide a particularly helpful and practical form of introduction to writers whose works are extensive or which present special problems for the modern reader, who can then proceed with a sense of his bearings and an informed eye for the writer's art.

An important feature of these books is the extensive reference list of the author's works and the descriptive list of the most useful biographies, commentaries and critical studies.

Acknowledgments

The extracts from *Billy Budd* use the text edited by Frederic Barron Freeman and corrected by Elizabeth Treeman. Copyright 1948, 1956, by the President and Fellows of Harvard College. By permission of Harvard University Press.

The other extracts are based on the original editions.

Contents

CONTENTS

Chronological table

1819   Birth of Herman Melville, 1 August, New York; Birth of Walt Whitman.

1830   Allan Melville, Herman's father, goes bankrupt.

1832   Death of Allan Melville.

1832–37   Melville attends various schools, works for different relatives.

1837   Melville becomes a school-teacher; Hawthorne's *Twice-Told Tales*, Emerson's *The American Scholar* published.

1839   Melville serves as cabin-boy on the *St. Lawrence*, bound for Liverpool.

1840 (December)   Melville joins the whaling-ship *Acushnet*; Dana's *Two Years Before the Mast*.

1841   Melville on the whaling voyage; Emerson's *Essays* (First Series).

1842 (July)   Melville deserts ship at Nukuheva.
July–August   Lives with the Typee, three-four weeks.
September–October   In Tahiti.

1843   Melville joins the U.S. Navy frigate *United States*.

1844   Arrives in America.

1845   *Typee* written.

1846   *Omoo* written.

1847 Melville marries Elizabeth Shaw, settles in New York.

1848 *Mardi* written.

1849 *Redburn* and *White-Jacket* written; Visit to England in October.

1850 *Moby Dick* written;
September Melville buys farm at Pittsfield, Massachusetts, near Hawthorne; Hawthorne's *The Scarlet Letter* published.

1852 *Pierre* published.

1853 'Bartleby the Scrivener' published in *Putnam's Monthly Magazine*.

1854 *Israel Potter* serialised in *Putnam's*.

1855 'Benito Cereno' published in *Putnam's*.

1856 Melville sails to Europe; *The Confidence-Man* written; *Piazza Tales* ('Bartleby', 'Benito Cereno' and other pieces) published.

1857 Journey through the Holy Land.

1858–59 Three American lecture-tours.

1860 Cruise on the *Meteor*, captained by his brother, Thomas.

1861 American Civil War.

1862 Melville sells his farm, returns to New York.

1866 Melville appointed customs inspector; *Battle Pieces* (poems) published privately.

1867 Malcolm, Melville's eldest son, shoots and kills himself.

1876 *Clarel* (a long poem) privately published.

1885 Melville retires.

1891 *Billy Budd* completed; Death of Melville 28 September.

1924 *Billy Budd* first published.

Herman Melville—his life and works

As the chronological table shows, Melville travelled extensively in his youth. His experiences then supplied the raw material for his novels. His inspiration, to begin with, was in the physical reality of his adventurous travels: shifting seascapes, glowing tropical scenes, the hard tack of shipboard life. The novels, while fully re-creating these actualities, go beyond documentary realism. Melville's imagination discloses latent meanings in the observed reality.

Melville in fact spent only about three years at sea, doing lowly jobs. Some recent criticism has disparaged his supposed expert knowledge and questioned the authenticity of his accounts as records of personal experience. As he must, for instance, have had a humble position on the *United States*, could he have known Jack Chase as familiarly as he claims in *White-Jacket*? In any case, was Jack quite the heroic figure in fact that Melville makes him out to be? Then again, it is quite easily established that for much of the background to his novels Melville drew not on his own experience but on travel-books, histories, articles.

These queries concern irrelevancies. The real issue is what Melville made of his material, wherever he found it. His experience at sea no doubt gave life to what he took at second-hand. But he had the sort of mind which takes inspiration from documents, illustrations, journals, as easily as from living reality. 'Benito Cereno', based upon Captain Delano's *Voyages*, shows how Melville can transform factual chronicle into minutely visualised action, dialogue and dramatic conflict of great moral tension. Though scholarship can identify the borrowings, the novels give no sense of discontinuity between what Melville took from his reading and what he knew from personal experience.

Similarly, the imaginative design of the novels fuses into unity facts, invented incidents, characters and events altered from their originals. To appreciate what Melville is about, we must widen our understanding both of 'experience' and of 'fact'. For Melville, experience was every contact between him and the world around him, fact the woman starving to death in Liverpool seen by Redburn—or the impression made by this on the observing mind.

Melville did not for long rest content with recording the sort of experience which won him his first audience: hazardous travel, exotic scenes, the surface of events. The geographical journey became a spiritual quest. Melville embarked on his unending exploration of human destiny, of man's route through the appalling confusions of his world.

His search brought him no certainty. Man and his world remained enigmatic, the Christian God an arbitrary begetter of suffering and loss. Good, in the affairs of life, had no advantage over evil, nor was it paramount in man. So, through the experiences of White-Jacket, Ishmael, Benito Cereno, who look for certainty amongst deceitful appearances, Melville dramatised his bleak reckoning of humanity's struggle with itself and its at best neutral environment. The ordeals and illusions of Ahab are those of mankind; the imagery of seas and islands, of the savagery and tranquillity of Nature symbolise the conflicting impulses in human beings and their society and characterise the equivocal nature of their God.

His own life gave him no taste of certainty. His father's bankruptcy, his own brief triumph and long years of failure and obscurity all substantiated the sombre lessons of his Calvinist upbringing. These experiences gave a personal impetus to his ideas, though the novels develop them far beyond their purely individual relevance. But again, what he writes has been 'experienced'. Melville is not Bartleby, but he is intimate with the feelings Bartleby endures. In the same way, however deeply Melville plunges in his metaphysical searchings, his scenes maintain their actuality. They are physically present. So too his characters, whatever their symbolic role, move before us as plausible human beings.

Melville was out of sympathy with the spirit of his age and with most of its literary celebrities. He enjoyed a short companionship with Hawthorne, which helped shape *Moby Dick*. Apart from that, he was a solitary worker, experimenting on his own with the techniques by which he could make the novel express his vision.

His novels are consequently, in form and manner, unorthodox: exotic blends of fact and fiction, narrative and philosophy, precise, circumstantial prose and poetical rhapsodies. The stories are basically simple, set down in chronological sequence. But events, settings, characters bear a load of implication, inter-related by recurrent images and the cross-bearings of sequence upon sequence. No one part or aspect of the novel gives a handy abridgment of its 'meaning'. The statement of meaning is the whole novel. We must therefore guard against taking the narrator's words alone as expressing Melville's opinions, a particular temptation with Melville, so much being autobiographical and often told in the first person.

For these reasons, interpretations of Melville are diverse.

He is difficult to pin down. If much of his thought was tormented, there are gusto, enthusiasm and humour as well, an appetite for experiencing the variety of life. But he gave no final answer to his riddles. We cannot encapsule his views. His interest was more in rendering the paradoxes of life than in resolving them. Terror and joy, ugliness and beauty, evil and good live together. Melville's insistence was on the terror, but not to the point of imbalance and obsession.

Scheme of extracts

The following extracts are in chronological order; at appropriate points the commentary explains what was happening in Melville's life and how it bears upon his work.

Each of the sections illustrates the general character of Melville's writing at its particular period. The features demonstrated in the first did not, of course, disappear. They were the foundation on which Melville built, refining their mode of expression and extending their range. The ensuing sections each take one central aspect of Melville's art as it appears in a major work.

Within this framework the extracts illustrate not only that aspect but the various facets of Melville's technique and thought which it involves. Thus the third section takes into account not just the psychological study of Bartleby and Benito Cereno but the total situation which has brought about their collapse, and the means by which Melville defines it.

Generally, the commentary turns on the various aspects of Melville's art which each of the extracts demonstrates. It links these with the particular topic of each section, with Melville's development as a novelist and the recurrence and modifications of his main themes and images. Development and change there were. But perhaps what the chronological presentation brings out most clearly is the underlying integrity of Melville's attitudes. The hopeful humanitarian became the sceptical enquirer; the compassion and honesty never died.

Early novels: narrative, ideas, characterisation

Narrative and the exposition of ideas

Melville intended *Typee* as an authentic record of the time he spent as guest-captive of the Typees, a cannibal tribe in the Marquesas islands. Tom, the first-person narrator, is Melville himself. No doubt he heightened and edited the facts of his experience. He drew on various books to supplement his own observations and memories. He exaggerated the length of his stay. But essentially, *Typee* is true to the imaginative impact of what Melville saw, felt and thought.

Despite an occasional undertone of menace and danger, it emphasises the idyllic simplicity of primitive life and presents the Typees as 'noble savages'. The picture does not stand up to cold examination. The Marquesas islands were not really an Eden, nor their inhabitants fundamentally more innocent than any other humans. Melville was responding emotionally to the beauty of exotic scenes and the novelty of unfamiliar customs. Nukuheva became a romantic metaphor to set against the anxieties, hypocrisies and 'go-getting' crudities of nineteenth-century America. The basic contrast in *Typee* is between western civilisation and the primitive society of the South Sea islands, to the detriment of the former.

The Typees themselves had so far escaped the effects of trading and missionary enterprise. The following passage describes the fate in store for them, apparent wherever else the Europeans had established themselves. Melville's humanitarian feelings rebelled against the islanders' degradation by a supposedly superior race, complacent in its hypocritical sense of mission.

I

The penalty of the Fall presses very lightly upon the valley of Typee; for, with the one solitary exception of striking a light, I scarcely saw any piece of work performed there which caused the sweat to stand upon a single brow. As for digging and delving for a livelihood, the thing is altogether unknown . . . How little do some of these poor islanders comprehend when they look around them, that no inconsiderable part of their disasters originates in certain tea-party excitements, under the influence of which benevolent-looking gentlemen in white cravats solicit alms, and old ladies in spectacles, and young ladies in sober russet low gowns, contribute sixpences towards the creation of a fund, the object of which is to ameliorate the spiritual condition of the Polynesians, but whose end has almost invariably been to accomplish their temporal destruction!

Let the savages be civilized, but civilize them with benefits, and not with evils; and let heathenism be destroyed, but not by destroying the heathen. The Anglo-Saxon hive have extirpated Paganism from the greater part of the North American continent; but with it they have likewise extirpated the greater portion of the Red race. Civilization is gradually sweeping from the earth the lingering vestiges of Paganism, and at the same time the shrinking forms of its unhappy worshippers.

Among the islands of Polynesia, no sooner are the images overturned, the temples demolished, and the idolaters converted into *nominal* Christians, than disease, vice, and premature death make their appearance. The depopulated land is then recruited from the rapacious hordes of enlightened individuals who settle themselves within its borders, and clamorously announce the progress of the Truth. Neat villas, trim gardens, shaven lawns, spires, and cupolas arise, while the poor savage soon finds himself an interloper in the country of his fathers, and that too on the very site of the hut where he was born. The spontaneous fruits of the earth, which God in his wisdom had ordained for the support of the indolent natives, remorselessly seized upon and appropriated by the stranger, are devoured before the eyes of the starving inhabitants, or sent on board the numerous vessels which now touch at their shores.

When the famished wretches are cut off in this manner from their natural supplies, they are told by their benefactors to work and earn their support by the sweat of their brows! But to no fine gentleman born to hereditary opulence does manual labour come more unkindly than to the luxurious Indian when thus robbed of the bounty of Heaven. Habituated to a life of indolence, he cannot and will not exert himself; and want, disease, and vice, all evils of foreign growth, soon terminate his miserable existence.

But what matters all this? Behold the glorious result!— The abominations of Paganism have given way to the pure rites of the Christian worship, the ignorant savage has been supplanted by the refined European! Look at Honolulu, the metropolis of the Sandwich Islands!—A community of disinterested merchants, and devoted self-exiled heralds of the Cross, located on the very spot that twenty years ago was defiled by the presence of idolatry. What a subject for an eloquent Bible-meeting orator! Nor has such an opportunity for a display of missionary rhetoric been allowed to pass by unimproved!—But when these philanthropists send us such glowing accounts of one half of their labours, why does their modesty restrain them from publishing the other half of the good they have wrought?—Not until I visited

Honolulu was I aware of the fact that the small remnant of the natives had been civilized into draught horses, and evangelized into beasts of burden. But so it is. They have been literally broken into the traces, and are harnessed to the vehicles of their spiritual instructors like so many dumb brutes!

Among[1] a multitude of similar exhibitions that I saw, I shall never forget a robust, red-faced, and very lady-like personage, a missionary's spouse, who day after day for months together took her regular airings in a little go-cart drawn by two of the islanders, one an old grey-headed man, and the other a roguish stripling, both being, with the exception of the fig-leaf, as naked as when they were born. Over a level piece of ground this pair of *draught* bipeds would go with a shambling, unsightly trot, the youngster hanging back all the time like a knowing horse, while the old hack plodded on and did all the work.

Rattling along through the streets of the town in this stylish equipage, the lady looks about her as magnificently as any queen driven in state to her coronation. A sudden elevation, and a sandy road however, soon disturb her serenity. The small wheels become imbedded on the loose soil,—the old stager stands tugging and sweating, while the young one frisks about and does nothing; not an inch does the chariot budge. Will the tender-hearted lady, who has left friends and home for the good of the souls of the poor heathen, will she think a little about their bodies and get out, and ease the wretched old man until the ascent is mounted? Not she; she could not dream of it. To be sure, she used to think nothing of driving the cows to pasture on the old farm in New England; but times have changed since then. So she retains her seat and bawls out, 'Hookee! hookee!' (Pull, pull.) The old gentleman, frightened at the sound, labours away harder than ever; and the younger one makes a great show of straining himself, but takes care to keep one eye on his mistress, in order to know when to dodge out of harm's way. At last the good lady loses all

[1] Some editions do not contain the following passage.

patience; 'Hookee! hookee!' and rap goes the heavy handle
of her huge fan over the naked skull of the old savage;
while the young one shies to one side and keeps beyond its
range. 'Hookee! hookee!' again she cries—'Hookee tata
kannaka!' (Pull strong, men,)—but all in vain, and she is
obliged in the end to dismount and, sad necessity! actually
to walk to the top of the hill.

Typee, ch. 26

The passage is bluntly sardonic: 'the glorious result', 'the
pure rites of Christian worship', 'devoted self-exiled
heralds'. Melville builds up a series of bitter contrasts: between the islanders' wretchedness and the missionaries'
comforts; between the proclaimed and the unpublicised
effects (and methods) of introducing Christianity. Specify
some of these contrasts and comment on their effectiveness. Do they actualise the charges Melville is making
against 'the Anglo-Saxon hive'?

Melville enlivens his accusations with satirical glimpses
of individual self-deception and folly: narrative supple-
ments the general exposition. So the conduct of the 'robust,
red-faced' wife mocks the nicely-observed missionary re-
finements at home. Does the concluding anecdote strengthen
Melville's criticism? How does he convey his opinion of the
missionary's wife? For example, how does her behaviour
contradict some of the words Melville uses to describe her?

After *Omoo*, which continues the story of Melville's
South Seas adventures, Melville wrote *Mardi*, an allegorical
novel so different from its predecessors that it lost him his
popularity. His next two novels, *Redburn* and *White-Jacket*,
return to his realistic manner. *Redburn*, like *Typee* a quasi-
autobiography told in the first person, is based on Melville's
first voyage. The passage to England greatly moderates Redburn's romantic enthusiasm for life at sea, as it had
Melville's. Like Melville, he is cut off by birth and up-

bringing from his companions. The crew are vicious and brutal, dominated by a sinister seaman called Jackson, diseased and malevolent. The Liverpool slums appal the young American; after some fictional and inconclusive escapades in London, Redburn/Melville is glad to re-embark for home.

For all its miseries, shipboard life has the value of testing the individual's endurance. Innocence encounters evil. The ship and its complement reflect society. They are a microcosm of life itself, stripping civilisation to its essential passions. Here, Melville's pity and reformist zeal champion the oppressed in his own society. His feelings, arising naturally from the events, move into the wider dimensions of social life. The simple concrete prose cuts away the whimsies and fake elegance of much of *Typee*. The following passage describes the fever which ravages the steerage passengers on the voyage home; and draws its conclusions.

2

On the second day, seven died, one of whom was the little tailor; on the third, four; on the fourth, six, of whom one was the Greenland sailor, and another, a woman in the cabin, whose death, however, was afterward supposed to have been purely induced by her fears. These last deaths brought the panic to its height; and sailors, officers, cabin passengers, and emigrants, all looked upon each other like lepers. All but the only true leper among us—the mariner Jackson, who seemed elated with the thought that for *him* —already in the deadly clutches of another disease—no danger was to be apprehended from a fever which only swept off the comparatively healthy. Thus, in the midst of the despair of the healthful, this incurable invalid was not cast down; not, at least, by the same considerations that appalled the rest.

And still, beneath a gray, gloomy sky, the doomed craft

beat on; now on this tack, now on that; battling against hostile blasts, and drenched in rain and spray; scarcely making an inch of progress toward her port.

On the sixth morning, the weather merged into a gale, to which we stripped our ship to a storm-stay-sail. In ten hours' time, the waves ran in mountains; and the *Highlander* rose and fell like some vast buoy on the water. Shrieks and lamentations were driven to leeward, and drowned in the roar of the wind among the cordage; while we gave to the gale the blackened bodies of five more of the dead. . . .

At midnight the wind went down; leaving a long, rolling sea; and, for the first time in a week, a clear, starry sky.

In the first morning-watch I sat with Harry on the windlass, watching the billows; which, seen in the night, seemed real hills, upon which fortresses might have been built; and real valleys, in which villages, and groves, and gardens, might have nestled. It was like a landscape in Switzerland; for down into those dark, purple glens, often tumbled the white foam of the wave-crests, like avalanches; while the seething and boiling that ensued seemed the swallowing up of human beings.

By the afternoon of the next day this heavy sea subsided; and we bore down on the waves, with all our canvas set; stun'-sails alow and aloft; and our best steersman at the helm; the captain himself at his elbow;—bowling along, with a fair, cheering breeze over the taffrail. . . .

However this narrative of the circumstances attending the fever among the emigrants on the *Highlander* may appear; and though these things happened so long ago; yet such events, nevertheless, are perhaps taking place to-day. But the only account you obtain of such events is generally contained in a newspaper paragraph, under the shipping-head. *There* is the obituary of the destitute dead, who die on the sea. They die, like the billows that break on the shore, and no more are heard or seen. But in the events, thus merely initialized in the catalogue of passing occurrences, and but glanced at by the readers of news, who are more taken up with paragraphs of fuller flavor;

what a world of life and death, what a world of humanity and its woes, lies shrunk into a three-worded sentence!

You see no plague-ship driving through a stormy sea; you hear no groans of despair; you see no corpses thrown over the bulwarks; you mark not the wringing hands and torn hair of widows and orphans:—all is a blank. And one of these blanks I have but filled up, in recounting the details of the *Highlander's* calamity.

Besides that natural tendency, which hurries into oblivion the last woes of the poor; other causes combine to suppress the detailed circumstances of disasters like these. Such things, if widely known, operate unfavorably to the ship, and make her a bad name; and to avoid detention at quarantine, a captain will state the case in the most palliating light, and strive to hush it up, as much as he can.

In no better place than this, perhaps, can a few words be said, concerning emigrant ships in general.

Let us waive that agitated national topic, as to whether such multitudes of foreign poor should be landed on our American shores; let us waive it, with the one only thought, that if they can get here, they have God's right to come; though they bring all Ireland and her miseries with them. For the whole world is the patrimony of the whole world; there is no telling who does not own a stone in the Great Wall of China. But we waive all this; and will only consider how best the emigrants can come hither, since come they do, and come they must and will.

Of late, a law has been passed in Congress, restricting ships to a certain number of emigrants, according to a certain rate. If this law were enforced, much good might be done; and so also might much good be done, were the English law likewise enforced concerning the fixed supply of food for every emigrant embarking from Liverpool. But it is hardly to be believed that either of these laws is observed.

But in all respects, no legislation, even nominally, reaches the hard lot of the emigrant. What ordinance makes it obligatory upon the captain of a ship, to supply the steer-

14

age passengers with decent lodgings, and give them light and air in that foul den, where they are immured during a long voyage across the Atlantic? What ordinance necessitates him to place the *galley*, or steerage passengers' stove, in a dry place of shelter, where the emigrants can do their cooking during a storm, or wet weather? What ordinance obliges him to give them more room on deck, and let them have an occasional run fore and aft? There is no law concerning these things. And if there was, who but some Howard[2] in office would see it enforced? and how seldom is there a Howard in office!

Redburn, ch. 58

The raging fever; the raging storm: is this too glib? Or does the implied connection discreetly emphasise the general mood? Consider how the connection is implied. The penultimate paragraph of the narrative adds immensely to the visual force of the rather commonplace, 'the waves ran in mountains': by relating the livid, tumbling ocean to the details of 'a landscape in Switzerland'. Which of these details links the storm to the dying emigrants? What earlier detail in the sounds also supplies a link?

We shift from the particularised shipboard scenes (what details stick in your mind?) to the appeal for reform. The first two paragraphs of Melville's commentary provide a transition, full of vivid particulars, as is the call for reform. Melville does not ask for abstractions—'safety', 'comfort'— but for 'decent lodgings', 'a dry place for shelter', and so on. The passage as a whole makes up a unified sequence. Do all its parts contribute to its effectiveness as argument? Where and how does Melville go beyond the issue of emigrants' hardships? Is it the appeal for specific reform

[2] John Howard (1726–90), the celebrated English penal reformer, notably persistent in urging the effective administration of the reforming Acts for whose passage he was largely responsible.

that remains with you from the passage, or any other impression?

Boarding the U.S. frigate *Neversink*, White-Jacket, the narrator, is Melville embarking on the *United States* in Hawaii. During the voyage he fluctuates from rather vacuous bonhomie to penetrating despair. His views, too, are strangely inconsistent: he praises democracy, then castigates it as mob rule; sees infinite possibilities for good in mankind, then ineradicable evil. Melville was approaching the sombre vision of his later books, still not wholly apprehended, still seeking full artistic expression; and so, like White-Jacket's character, unintegrated.

The following broadly satirical portrait of Cuticle moves unexpectedly to quite another world. Melville seems here, forgetting White-Jacket, to speak as himself.

3

Cadwallader Cuticle, M.D., and Honorary Member of the most distinguished Colleges of Surgeons both in Europe and America, was our Surgeon of the Fleet. Nor was he at all blind to the dignity of his position; to which, indeed, he was rendered peculiarly competent, if the reputation he enjoyed was deserved. He had the name of being the foremost surgeon in the Navy, a gentleman of remarkable science and a veteran practitioner.

He was a small, withered man, nearly, perhaps quite, sixty years of age. His chest was shallow, his shoulders bent, his pantaloons hung round skeleton legs, and his face was singularly attenuated. In truth, the corporeal vitality of this man seemed, in a good degree, to have died out of him. He walked abroad, a curious patchwork of life and death, with a wig, one glass eye, and a set of false teeth, while his voice was husky and thick; but his mind seemed undebilitated as in youth; it shone out of his remaining eye with basilisk brilliancy.

16

Like most old physicians and surgeons who have seen much service, and have been promoted to high professional place for their scientific attainments, this Cuticle was an enthusiast in his calling. In private, he had once been heard to say, confidentially, that he would rather cut off a man's arm than dismember the wing of the most delicate pheasant. In particular, the department of Morbid Anatomy was his peculiar love; and in his state-room below he had a most unsightly collection of Parisian casts, in plaster and wax, representing all imaginable malformations of the human members, both organic and induced by disease. Chief among these was a cast, often to be met with in the Anatomical Museums of Europe, and no doubt an unexaggerated copy of a genuine original; it was the head of an elderly woman, with an aspect singularly gentle and meek, but at the same time wonderfully expressive of a gnawing sorrow, never to be relieved. You would almost have thought it the face of some abbess, for some unspeakable crime voluntarily sequestered from human society, and leading a life of agonized penitence without hope, so marvellously sad and tearfully pitiable was this head. But when you first beheld it, no such emotions ever crossed your mind. All your eyes and all your horrified soul were fast fascinated and frozen by the sight of a hideous, crumpled horn, like that of a ram, downward growing out from the forehead, and partly shadowing the face; but as you gazed, the freezing fascination of its horribleness gradually waned, and then your whole heart burst with sorrow, as you contemplated those aged features, ashy, pale and wan. The horn seemed the mark of a curse for some mysterious sin, conceived and committed before the spirit had entered the flesh. Yet that sin seemed something imposed and not voluntarily sought; some sin growing out of the heartless necessities of the predestination of things; some sin under which the sinner sank in sinless woe.

White-Jacket, ch. 61

17

The grotesque head, innocent and blemished, symbolises human anguish, punishment at once undeserved and manifesting an inborn human evil. The echoing final phrase touches on the whole mystery of human guilt, innocence and suffering, paradoxically united. Melville goes beyond matters of morality or social justice to the metaphysical questionings of his mature novels. It could come, almost, anywhere in Melville. Yet his experiences on the *United States-Neversink*—storms, routine chores, floggings, human desperation and human companionship—give it an immediate as well as a universal validity.

The following passage may act as sequel to the preceding, for it shows Cuticle in action; and, perhaps, some of the background of experience to Melville's feelings. *White-Jacket*'s ostensible purpose was to expose the inhuman practices common on U.S. Navy ships. In this, in its unsparing realism, it follows the tradition of R. H. Dana's *Two Years Before the Mast*, which Melville greatly admired. Whatever the dilemmas in Melville's mind as he advanced from personal experiences into the spiritual enigmas of life, he retains here his deep humanitarianism, plainly evident in the documentary starkness of this extract. Though the incident is imagined—no such operation was performed on Melville's voyage—its realism is unquestionable.

4

Here was a sailor, who, four days previous, had stood erect —a pillar of life—with an arm like a royal-mast, and a thigh like a windlass. But the slightest conceivable finger-touch of a bit of crooked trigger had eventuated in stretching him out, more helpless than an hour-old babe, with a blasted thigh, utterly drained of its brawn. And who was it that now stood over him like a superior being, and, as if clothed himself with the attributes of immortality, indifferently discoursed of carving up his broken flesh, and thus piecing out his abbreviated days? Who was it, that, in capacity of Surgeon, seemed enacting the part of a Regenerator of life? The withered, shrunken, one-eyed, toothless, hairless Cuticle; with a trunk half dead—a *memento mori* to behold! . . .

'Mr. Surgeon of the Fleet,' said Surgeon Bandage, 'if you are about to lecture, permit me to present you with your teeth; they will make your discourse more readily understood.' And so saying, Bandage, with a bow, placed the two semicircles of ivory into Cuticle's hands.

'Thank you, Surgeon Bandage,' said Cuticle, and slipped the ivory into its place.

'In the first place, now, young gentlemen, let me direct your attention to the excellent preparation before you. I have had it unpacked from its case, and set up here from my stateroom, where it occupies the spare berth; and all this for your express benefit, young gentlemen. This skeleton I procured in person from the Hunterian Department of the Royal College of Surgeons in London. It is a masterpiece of art. But we have no time to examine it now. Delicacy forbids that I should amplify at a juncture like this'—casting an almost benignant glance toward the patient, now beginning to open his eyes; 'but let me point out to you upon this thigh-bone'—disengaging it from the skeleton, with a gentle twist—'the precise place where I propose to perform the operation. *Here*, young gentlemen, *here* is the place. You perceive it is very near the point of articulation with the trunk.'

'Yes,' interposed Surgeon Wedge, rising on his toes, 'yes, young gentlemen, the point of articulation with the *acetabulum* of the *os innominatum*.'

'Where's your *Bell on Bones*, Dick?' whispered one of the assistants to the student next him. 'Wedge has been spending the whole morning over it, getting out the hard names.'

'Surgeon Wedge,' said Cuticle, looking round severely, 'we will dispense with your commentaries, if you please, at present. Now, young gentlemen, you cannot but perceive, that the point of operation being so near the trunk and the vitals, it becomes an unusually beautiful one, demanding a steady hand and a true eye; and, after all, the patient may die under my hands.'

'Quick, Steward! water, water; he's fainting again!' cried the two messmates.

'Don't be alarmed for your comrade, men,' said Cuticle, turning round. 'I tell you it is not an uncommon thing for the patient to betray some emotion upon these occasions —most usually manifested by swooning; it is quite natural it should be so. But we must not delay the operation. Steward, that knife—no, the next one—there, that's it. He is coming to, I think'—feeling the top-man's wrist. 'Are you all ready, sir?'

This last observation was addressed to one of the *Neversink's* assistant surgeons, a tall, lank, cadaverous young man, arrayed in a sort of shroud of white canvas, pinned about his throat, and completely enveloping his person. He was seated on a match-tub—the skeleton swinging near his head—at the foot of the table, in readiness to grasp the limb, as when a plank is being severed by a carpenter and his apprentice.

'The sponges, steward,' said Cuticle, for the last time taking out his teeth, and drawing up his shirt sleeve still further. Then, taking the patient by the wrist, 'Stand by, now, you messmates; keep hold of his arms; pin him down. Steward, put your hand on the artery; I shall commence as soon as his pulse begins to—*now, now!*' Letting fall the wrist, feeling the thigh carefully, and bowing over it an instant, he drew the fatal knife unerringly across the flesh. As it first touched the part, the row of surgeons simultaneously dropped their eyes to the watches in their hands, while the patient lay, with eyes horribly distended, in a kind of waking trance. Not a breath was heard; but as the quivering flesh parted in a long, lingering gash, a spring of blood welled up between the living walls of the wound, and two thick streams, in opposite directions, coursed

20

down the thigh. The sponges were instantly dipped in the purple pool; every face present was pinched to a point with suspense; the limb writhed; the man shrieked; his messmates pinioned him; while round and round the leg went the unpitying cut.

'The saw!' said Cuticle.

Instantly it was in his hand.

Full of the operation, he was about to apply it, when, looking up, and turning to the assistant surgeons, he said, 'Would any of you young gentlemen like to apply the saw? A splendid subject!'

Several volunteered; when, selecting one, Cuticle surrendered the instrument to him, saying, 'Don't be hurried, now; be steady.'

While the rest of the assistants looked upon their comrade with glances of envy, he went rather timidly to work; and Cuticle, who was earnestly regarding him, suddenly snatched the saw from his hand. 'Away, butcher! you disgrace the profession. Look at *me*.'

For a few moments the thrilling rasping sound was heard; and then the top-man seemed parted in twain at the hip, as the leg slowly slid into the arms of the pale, gaunt man in the shroud, who at once made away with it, and tucked it out of sight under one of the guns.

White-Jacket, ch. 63

Himself, ironically, decayed with age, Cuticle 'indifferently discoursed' of his patient, seemingly less to him than the skeleton—it, not the man, 'is a masterpiece of art'. The top-man becomes an inanimate object, his leg a plank. How else does Melville convey this impression? There is a hint of sadism in Cuticle's delaying the operation until the top-man is conscious, though Melville makes no direct inference; nor ever talks specifically of cruelty. The passage makes its points by implication: by the repeated paradox of death where life should be, life where death (Cuticle's physique, the 'sort of shroud of canvas', 'the living walls of the wound'); by the swift sequence of gory details, exciting every sense ('the thrilling rasping sound'); by the black humour of Cuticle's ludicrous posturings. Here, the narrative *embodies* the ideas. How does this differ from the *Typee* and *Redburn* extracts? Examine the details by which Melville makes his points in this passage : and say in which direction the episode would be likely to drive his ideas.

Since setting sail, White-Jacket has witnessed many brutal floggings. (During Melville's voyage there were over 160, mostly for trivial misdeeds.) Not only their physical, but their psychological, damage has shocked him, and his own threatened degradation (again an imagined incident) releases unsuspected impulses. Jack Chase, one of his saviours here, was a real sailor who impressed Melville profoundly, becoming a symbol of frank, honourable manliness—one of the few evidences of good he took from the *United States*—and, in his reincarnations in later books, of the principle of human good ensnared with evil.

5

I had now been on board the frigate upward of a year, and remained unscourged; the ship was homeward bound, and in a few weeks, at most, I would be a free man. And now, after making a hermit of myself in some things, in order to avoid the possibility of the scourge, here it was hanging over me for a thing utterly unforeseen, for a crime of which I was utterly innocent. But all that was as nought. I saw that my case was hopeless; my solemn disclaimer was thrown in my teeth, and the boatswain's mate stood curling his fingers through the *cat*.

There are times when wild thoughts enter a man's heart, when he seems almost irresponsible for his act and his deed. The captain stood on the weather-side of the deck. Sideways, on an unobstructed line with him, was the opening of the lee-gangway, where the side-ladders are suspended in port. Nothing but a slight bit of sinnate-stuff served to rail in this opening, which was cut right down to the level of the captain's feet, showing the far sea beyond. I stood a little to windward of him, and, though he was a large, powerful man, it was certain that a sudden rush against him, along the slanting deck, would infallibly pitch him head-foremost into the ocean, though he who so rushed must needs go over with him. My blood seemed clotting in my veins; I felt icy cold at the tips of my fingers, and a dimness was before my eyes. But through that dimness the boatswain's mate, scourge in hand, loomed like a giant, and Captain Claret, and the blue sea seen through the opening at the gangway, showed with an awful vividness. I cannot analyze my heart, though it then stood still within me. But the thing that swayed me to my purpose was not altogether the thought that Captain Claret was about to degrade me, and that I had taken an oath with my soul that he should not. No, I felt my man's manhood so bottomless within me, that no word, no blow, no scourge of Captain Claret could cut me deep enough for that. I but swung to an instinct in me—the instinct diffused through all animated nature, the same that prompts even a worm to turn under the heel. Locking souls with him, I meant to drag Captain Claret from this earthly tribunal of his to that of Jehovah, and let Him decide between us. No other way could I escape the scourge.

Nature has not implanted any power in man that was not meant to be exercised at times, though too often our powers have been abused. The privilege, inborn and inalienable, that every man has, of dying himself, and inflicting death upon another, was not given to us without a purpose. These are the last resources of an insulted and unendurable existence.

'To the gratings, sir!' said Captain Claret; 'do you hear?'

My eye was measuring the distance between him and the sea.

'Captain Claret,' said a voice advancing from the crowd.

I turned to see who this might be, that audaciously interposed at a juncture like this. It was the same remarkably handsome and gentlemanly corporal of marines, Colbrook, who has been previously alluded to, in the chapter describing killing time in a man-of-war.

'I know that man,' said Colbrook, touching his cap, and speaking in a mild, firm, but extremely deferential manner; 'and I know that he would not be found absent from his station, if he knew where it was.'

This speech was almost unprecedented. Seldom or never before had a marine dared to speak to the captain of a frigate in behalf of a seaman at the mast. But there was something so unostentatiously commanding in the calm manner of the man, that the captain, though astounded, did not in any way reprimand him. The very unusualness of his interference seemed Colbrook's protection.

Taking heart, perhaps from Colbrook's example, Jack Chase interposed, and in a manly but carefully respectful manner, in substance repeated the corporal's remark, adding that he had never found me wanting in the top.

Captain Claret looked from Chase to Colbrook, and from Colbrook to Chase—one the foremost man among the seamen, the other the foremost man among the soldiers—then all round on the packed and silent crew, and as if a slave to Fate, though supreme captain of a frigate, he turned to the first lieutenant, made some indifferent remark, and saying to me, *You may go*, sauntered aft into his cabin; while I, who in the desperation of my soul, had just escaped being a murderer and a suicide, almost burst into tears of thanksgiving where I stood.

White-Jacket, ch. 67

During the operation, White-Jacket is the de-personalised observer, his presence muted. Here he participates, involving us deeply, immediately in the action. His feelings shift the view from factual observation to his whirling impressions with the bosun's mate nightmarishly dominating the scene. Outwardly awaiting his fate, within White-Jacket finds his normal patterns of behaviour in collapse. It is an early example of Melville's penetrating behind events to innermost psychological responses. Is White-Jacket's account of the 'instinct' which prompted his feelings in place? How does it affect the narrative?

Melville's America nourished its optimistic faiths on expanding trade, technical inventiveness, limitless opportunity in a democracy freed of oppressive European traditions. Melville's contemporary, Emerson, notably optimistic, displayed great ingenuity in accommodating the theory to the many contrary facts of experience, such as an aggressively self-seeking capitalism and a powerless, poverty-stricken immigrant class.

Though keenly aware of the contradictions, Melville at first responded to Emerson's 'transcendental' philosophy and to the American Dream of the Utopia to which the nation's fresh start could lead. It was a noble and persuasive ideal, opening up new political and social prospects. The following passage pays eloquent tribute to it, in the context of a plea to abolish flogging in the American navy.

6

It is true that, during a long period of non-impressment, and even down to the present day, flogging has been, and still is, the law of the English navy. But in things of this kind England should be nothing to us, except an example to be shunned. Nor should wise legislators wholly govern themselves by precedents, and conclude that, since scourging has so long prevailed, some virtue must reside in it. Not so. The world has arrived at a period which renders it the part of Wisdom to pay homage to the prospective precedents of the Future, in preference to those of the Past. The Past is dead, and has no resurrection; but the Future is endowed with such a life, that it lives to us even in antici-

25

pation. The Past is, in many things, the foe of mankind; the Future is, in all things, our friend. In the Past is no hope; the Future is both hope and fruition. The Past is the text-book of tyrants; the Future the Bible of the Free. Those who are solely governed by the Past stand like Lot's wife, crystallized in the act of looking backward, and forever incapable of looking before.

Let us leave the Past, then, to dictate laws to immovable China; let us abandon it to the Chinese Legitimists of Europe. But for us, we will have another captain to rule over us—that captain who ever marches at the head of his troop, and beckons them forward, not lingering in the rear, and impeding their march with lumbering baggage-wagons of old precedents. *This* is the Past.

But in many things we Americans are driven to a rejection of the maxims of the Past, seeing that, ere long, the van of the nations must, of right, belong to ourselves. There are occasions when it is for America to make precedents, and not to obey them. We should, if possible, prove a teacher to posterity, instead of being the pupil of by-gone generations. More shall come after us than have gone before; the world is not yet middle-aged.

Escaped from the house of bondage, Israel of old did not follow after ways of the Egyptians. To her was given an express dispensation; to her were given new things under the sun. And we Americans are the peculiar, chosen people —the Israel of our time; we bear the ark of the liberties of the world. Seventy years ago we escaped from thrall; and, besides our first birthright—embracing one continent of earth—God has given to us, for a future inheritance, the broad domains of the political pagans, that shall yet come and lie down under the shade of our ark, without bloody hands being lifted. God has predestinated, mankind expects, great things from our race; and great things we feel in our souls. We are the pioneers of the world; the advance-guard, sent on through the wilderness of untried things, to break a new path in the New World that is ours. In our youth is our strength; in our inexperience our wisdom. At a period when other nations have but lisped, our deep voice is heard afar. Long enough have we been sceptics with regard to ourselves, and doubted whether, indeed, the political Messiah had come. But he has come in *us*, if we would but give utterance to his promptings. And let us always remember, that with ourselves, almost for the first time in the history of earth, national selfishness is unbounded philanthropy; for we cannot do a good to America, but we give alms to the world.

White-Jacket, ch. 36

Here again Melville drops the mask of White-Jacket, though he speaks now in a very different vein. The sentiment and the aphoristic style—'In our youth is our strength . . .'—are very Emersonian. The technique is oratorical, expressing broad, central ideas in readily comprehensible images, which, appropriately, often suggest movement, exploration, discovery: exemplify some of these images. There is vigour enough to convey Melville's confidence in the prospect of ameliorating the evils of life. Which do you find the more compelling generalisation, this or Extract 3?

Characterisation: external appearances

Melville was a perceptive, humorous observer of events and character. *White-Jacket* has its jolly shipboard performance of a rousing melodrama as well as the floggings; *The Confidence-Man* the lively bustle of its Mississippi riverboat passengers. America, as Melville's travels had shown him, was alive with eccentric humanity. It was the source, for Melville, of characters neatly defined by manner and appearance—like the 'supporting cast' of sailors in *Moby Dick*, identified with imaginative precision largely from the outside. The first extract describes the cabin-passengers on Redburn's return voyage.

27

7

One of them was an old fellow in a robust-looking coat, with broad skirts; he had a nose like a bottle of port wine; and would stand for a whole hour, with his legs straddling apart, and his hands deep down in his breeches pockets, as if he had two mints at work there, coining guineas. He was an abominable-looking old fellow, with cold, fat, jelly-like eyes; and avarice, heartlessness, and sensuality stamped all over him. He seemed all the time going through some process of mental arithmetic; doing sums with dollars and cents: his very mouth, wrinkled and drawn up at the corners, looked like a purse. When he dies, his skull ought to be turned into a savings box, with the till-hole between his teeth.

Another of the cabin inmates, was a middle-aged Londoner, in a comical Cockney-cut coat, with a pair of semicircular tails: so that he looked as if he were sitting in a swing. He wore a spotted neckerchief; a short, little, fiery-red vest; and striped pants, very thin in the calf, but very full about the waist. There was nothing describable about him but his dress; for he had such a meaningless face, I cannot remember it; though I have a vague impression that it looked at the time as if its owner was laboring under the mumps. Then there were two or three buckish-looking young fellows among the rest; who were all the time playing at cards on the poop, under the lee of the *spanker*; or smoking cigars on the taffrail; or sat quizzing the emigrant women with opera-glasses, levelled through the windows of the upper cabin. These sparks frequently called for the steward to help them to brandy and water, and talked about going on to Washington to see Niagara Falls.

There was also an old gentleman, who had brought with him three or four heavy files of the *London Times*, and other papers; and he spent all his hours in reading them, on the shady side of the deck, with one leg crossed over the other; and without crossed legs he never read at all. That was indispensable to the proper understanding of what he studied. He growled terribly, when disturbed by the sailors, who now and then were obliged to move him to get at the ropes.

Redburn, ch. 51

Melville has Dickens's ability to suggest character briefly in a *vignette* of significant features and habits. It depends on the extravagant invention which can imagine the 'old fellow's' hands coining guineas in his pocket. Such heightened similes describe, in a kind of shorthand, both physical appearance and personality. They give, of course, a stylised version of human psychology: each character has one characteristic. What do you learn about the cabin-passengers and how is this information conveyed?

Ishmael, the narrator of *Moby Dick*, comes to sign on the *Pequod*. Its owners, typical Yankee captains, are, however hard and grasping, Ishmael's last contact with normality before the *Pequod*'s wild odyssey under Captain Ahab. Ahab is recognisably of the same New England stock as Peleg and Bildad; but with him we are to reach, as we did briefly with White-Jacket, into the inner workings of the mind.

8

Now, Bildad, I am sorry to say, had the reputation of being an incorrigible old hunks, and in his sea-going days, a bitter, hard task-master. They told me in Nantucket, though it certainly seems a curious story, that when he sailed the old Categut whaleman, his crew, upon arriving home, were mostly all carried ashore to the hospital, sore exhausted and worn out. For a pious man, especially for a Quaker, he was certainly rather hard-hearted, to say the least. He never used to swear, though, at his men, they said; but somehow he got an inordinate quantity of cruel, unmiti-

29

gated hard work out of them. When Bildad was a chief-mate, to have his drab-colored eye intently looking at you, made you feel completely nervous, till you could clutch something—a hammer or a marling-spike, and go to work like mad, at something or other, never mind what. Indolence and idleness perished from before him. His own person was the exact embodiment of his utilitarian character. On his long, gaunt body, he carried no spare flesh, no superfluous beard, his chin having a soft, economical nap to it, like the worn nap of his broad-brimmed hat.

Such, then, was the person that I saw seated on the transom when I followed Captain Peleg down into the cabin. The space between the decks was small; and there, bolt-upright, sat old Bildad, who always sat so, and never leaned, and this to save his coat tails. His broad-brim was placed beside him; his legs were stiffly crossed; his drab vesture was buttoned up to his chin; and spectacles on nose, he seemed absorbed in reading from a ponderous volume.

'Bildad,' cried Captain Peleg, 'at it again, Bildad, eh? Ye have been studying those Scriptures, now, for the last thirty years, to my certain knowledge. How far ye got, Bildad?'

As if long habituated to such profane talk from his old shipmate, Bildad, without noticing his present irreverence, quietly looked up, and seeing me, glanced again inquiringly towards Peleg.

'He says he's our man, Bildad,' said Peleg, 'he wants to ship.'

'Dost thee?' said Bildad, in a hollow tone, and turning round to me.

'I *dost*,' said I unconsciously, he was so intense a Quaker.[1]

'What do ye think of him, Bildad?' said Peleg.

'He'll do,' said Bildad, eyeing me and then went on spelling away at his book in a mumbling tone quite audible . . .

Ashore, I had heard something of both Captain Peleg and

---

[1] i.e. in his use of second person singular.

his unaccountable old crony Bildad; how that they being the principal proprietors of the *Pequod*, therefore the other and more inconsiderable and scattered owners, left nearly the whole management of the ship's affairs to these two. And I did not know but what the stingy old Bildad might have a mighty deal to say about shipping hands, especially as I now found him on board the *Pequod*, quite at home there in the cabin, and reading his Bible as if at his own fireside. Now while Peleg was vainly trying to mend a pen with his jack-knife, old Bildad, to my no small surprise, considering that he was such an interested party in these proceedings; Bildad never heeded us, but went on mumbling to himself out of his book, '*Lay* not up for yourselves treasures upon earth, where moth—'

'Well, Captain Bildad,' interrupted Peleg, 'what d'ye say, what lay[2] shall we give this young man?'

'Thou knowest best,' was the sepulchral reply, 'the seven hundred and seventy-seventh wouldn't be too much, would it?—"where moth and rust do corrupt, but *lay*—"'

Moby Dick, ch. 16

Though longer and more elaborate, this is essentially the same kind of characterisation as in 7. What does it gain from the fuller treatment? Does the brief dialogue add anything to our awareness of the characters? Melville begins with a brief account of Bildad's appearance and character. How does the ensuing action support the description?

[2] The proportion of the profits paid to each hand.

'Moby Dick'—story into symbol

Redburn and *White-Jacket* restored Melville to the public favour which the allegorical fantasy of *Mardi* had extinguished. But *Moby Dick* met uncomprehending hostility. Melville, pushing forward into complex modes of thought and expression, had outgrown his audience. 'What I feel most moved to write,' he wrote to Hawthorne, 'that is banned—it will not pay. Yet, altogether, write the *other* way I cannot.'

Hawthorne and Melville shared, in Melville's words, 'that Calvinistic sense of Innate Depravity and Original Sin, from whose visitations . . . no deeply thinking mind is always and wholly free'; and Hawthorne's novels instructed Melville to keep symbol and allegory close to the substantial world of sensuous reality. Melville had already achieved this, notably in *White-Jacket*, where characters and incidents at times appear reflections of some cosmic struggle between good and evil. *Moby Dick* was to sustain it throughout an entire novel.

Melville's symbols grow from the visible facts of the *Pequod*'s voyage: the dying whales, the mess of blubber, the wood of the ship, the tossing waves. In the following extract, as the *Pequod* first enters milder waters, the sense of a heroic Quest emerges from the rendering of physical impressions.

Creation of mood

9

Some days elapsed, and ice and icebergs all astern, the *Pequod* now went rolling through the bright Quito[1] spring, which, at sea, almost perpetually reigns on the threshold of the eternal August of the Tropic. The warmly cool, clear, ringing, perfumed, overflowing, redundant days, were as crystal goblets of Persian sherbet, heaped up—flaked up, with rose-water snow. The starred and stately nights seemed haughty dames in jewelled velvets, nursing at home in lonely pride, the memory of their absent conquering Earls, the golden helmeted suns! For sleeping man, 'twas hard to choose between such winsome days and such seducing nights. But all the witcheries of that unwaning weather did not merely lend new spells and potencies to the outward world. Inward they turned upon the soul, especially when the still mild hours of eve came on; then, memory shot her crystals as the clear ice most forms of noiseless twilights. And all these subtle agencies, more and more they wrought on Ahab's texture.

Moby Dick, ch. 29

The mood of almost magical calm depends partly on the elaborate images (full of sense-impressions), partly on the echoing sounds. Pick out examples of each and show how they work together, as where the image in lines 6-7 embodies the qualities of the adjectives in lines 4-5.

'absent conquering Earls' suggests the adventuring knights of medieval Quests: something of this mood begins to call Ahab to his purposes, no ordinary whaling voyage, but one

[1] The capital of Ecuador, noted for its mild, balmy climate.

committed to revenge on the White Whale. The next passage, after Ahab has declared his purpose to the crew, charts the inception, nature and intensity of his mania.

Character and Symbolism

10

While the mate was getting the hammer, Ahab, without speaking, was slowly rubbing the gold piece against the skirts of his jacket, as if to heighten its lustre, and without using any words was meanwhile lowly humming to himself, producing a sound so strangely muffled and inarticulate that it seemed the mechanical humming of the wheels of his vitality in him.

Receiving the top-maul from Starbuck, he advanced towards the main-mast with the hammer uplifted in one hand, exhibiting the gold with the other, and with a high raised voice exclaiming: 'Whosoever of ye raises me a white-headed whale with a wrinkled brow and a crooked jaw; whosoever of ye raises me that white-headed whale, with three holes punctured in his starboard fluke—look ye, whosoever of ye raises me that same white whale, he shall have this gold ounce, my boys!'

'Huzza! huzza!' cried the seamen, as with swinging tarpaulins they hailed the act of nailing the gold to the mast.

'It's a white whale, I say,' resumed Ahab, as he threw down the top-maul; 'a white whale. Skin your eyes for him, men; look sharp for white water; if ye see but a bubble, sing out.'

All this while Tashtego, Daggoo, and Queequeg had looked on with even more intense interest and surprise than the rest, and at the mention of the wrinkled brow and crooked jaw they had started as if each was separately touched by some specific recollection.

'Captain Ahab,' said Tashtego, 'that white whale must be the same that some call Moby Dick.'

'Moby Dick?' shouted Ahab. 'Do ye know the white whale then, Tash?'

'Does he fan-tail a little curious, sir, before he goes down?' said the Gay-Header[2] deliberately.

'And has he a curious spout, too,' said Daggoo, 'very bushy, even for a parmacetty, and mighty quick, Captain Ahab?'

'And he have one, two, tree—oh! good many iron in him hide, too, Captain,' cried Queequeg disjointedly, 'all twisketee be-twisk, like him—him—' faltering hard for a word, and screwing his hand round and round as though uncorking a bottle—'like him—him—'

'Corkscrew!' cried Ahab, 'aye, Queequeg, the harpoons lie all twisted and wrenched in him; aye, Daggoo, his spout is a big one, like a whole shock of wheat, and white as a pile of our Nantucket wool after the great annual sheepshearing; aye, Tashtego, and he fan-tails like a split jib in a squall. Death and devils! men it is Moby Dick ye have seen—Moby Dick—Moby Dick!'

'Captain Ahab,' said Starbuck, who, with Stubb and Flask, had thus far been eyeing his superior with increasing surprise, but at last seemed struck with a thought which somehow explained all the wonder. 'Captain Ahab, I have heard of Moby Dick—but it was not Moby Dick that took off thy leg?' . . .

Moby Dick, ch. 36

Moby Dick had reaped away Ahab's leg, as a mower a blade of grass in the field. No turbaned Turk, no hired Venetian or Malay, could have smote him with more seeming malice. Small reason was there to doubt, then, that ever since that almost fatal encounter, Ahab had cherished a wild vindictiveness against the whale, all the more fell for that in his frantic morbidness he at last came to identify with him, not only all his bodily woes, but all his intellectual and spiritual exasperations. The White Whale swam before him as the monomaniac incarnation of all those malicious agencies which some deep men feel eating in

[2] Tashtego is an American Indian from Gay Head in New England.

them, till they are left living on with half a heart and half a lung. That intangible malignity which has been from the beginning; to whose dominion even the modern Christians ascribe one-half of the worlds; which the ancient Ophites of the east reverenced in their statue devil;—Ahab did not fall down and worship it like them; but deliriously transferring its idea to the abhorred White Whale, he pitted himself, all mutilated, against it. All that most maddens and torments; all that stirs up the lees of things; all truth with malice in it; all that cracks the sinews and cakes the brain; all the subtle demonisms of life and thought; all evil, to crazy Ahab, were visibly personified, and made practically assailable in Moby Dick. He piled upon the whale's white hump the sum of all the general rage and hate felt by his whole race from Adam down; and then, as if his chest had been a mortar, he burst his hot heart's shell upon it.

It is not probable that this monomania in him took its instant rise at the precise time of his bodily dismemberment. Then, in darting at the monster, knife in hand, he had but given loose to a sudden, passionate, corporal animosity; and when he received the stroke that tore him, he probably but felt the agonizing bodily laceration, but nothing more. Yet, when by this collision forced to turn towards home, and for long months of days and weeks, Ahab and anguish lay stretched together in one hammock, rounding in mid winter that dreary, howling Patagonian Cape; then it was, that his torn body and gashed soul bled into one another; and so interfusing, made him mad. That it was only then, on the homeward voyage, after the encounter, that the final monomania seized him, seems all but certain from the fact that, at intervals during the passage, he was a raving lunatic; and, though unlimbed of a leg, yet such vital strength yet lurked in his Egyptian chest, and was moreover intensified by his delirium, that his mates were forced to lace him fast, even there, as he sailed, raving in his hammock. In a strait-jacket, he swung to the mad rockings of the gales. And, when running into more sufferable latitudes, the ship, with mild stun' sails spread,

36

floated across the tranquil tropics, and, to all appearances, the old man's delirium seemed left behind him with the Cape Horn swells, and he came forth from his dark den into the blessed light and air; even then, when he bore that firm, collected front, however pale, and issued his calm orders once again; and his mates thanked God the direful madness was now gone; even then, Ahab, in his hidden self, raved on. Human madness is oftentimes a cunning and most feline thing. When you think it fled, it may have but become transfigured into some still subtler form. Ahab's full lunacy subsided not, but deepeningly contracted; like the unabated Hudson, when that noble Northman flows narrowly, but unfathomably through the Highland gorge. But, as in his narrow-flowing monomania, not one jot of Ahab's broad madness had been left behind; so in that broad madness, not one jot of his great natural intellect had perished. That before living agent, now became the living instrument. If such a furious trope may stand, his special lunacy stormed his general sanity, and carried it, and turned all its concentrated cannon upon its own mad mark; so that far from having lost his strength, Ahab, to that one end, did now possess a thousandfold more potency than ever he had sanely brought to bear upon any one reasonable object.

This is much; yet Ahab's larger, darker, deeper part remains unhinted. But vain to popularize profundities, and all truth is profound. Winding far down from within the very heart of this spiked Hôtel de Cluny where we here stand—however grand and wonderful, now quit it;—and take your way, ye nobler, sadder souls, to those vast Roman halls of Thermes,[3] where far beneath the fantastic towers of man's upper earth, his root of grandeur, his whole awful

[3] The remains of these 'halls' are in the vaults of the Cluny Museum (Hôtel de Cluny) in Paris. The museum occupies the site of the Roman Emperor Julian's thermal baths (French: *thermes*). Melville visited the Museum on 5 December 1849 and noted in his Journal: 'Descended into the vaults of the old Roman palace of Thermes. Baths, &c.'

essence sits in bearded state; an antique buried beneath antiquities, and throned on torsoes! So with a broken throne, the great gods mock that captive king; so like a Caryatid, he patient sits, upholding on his frozen brow the piled entablatures of ages. Wind ye down there, ye prouder, sadder souls! question that proud, sad king! A family like- ness! aye, he did beget ye, ye young exiled royalties; and from your grim sire only will the old State-secret come.

Moby Dick, ch. 41

The sailors respond to the offer of reward and the thrill of the chase; Moby Dick is simply an unusual whale. Ahab's feelings are more complex. Moby Dick has become the embodiment of 'all his intellectual and spiritual ex- asperations'; even of all the evil in the world. Yet Ahab's obsession is itself evil. But if evil, Ahab is also of 'great natural intellect', one of the 'deep men' sensitive to 'the subtle demonisms of life and thought'.

We begin here to understand Ahab's grandeur, his im- perial, indomitable will; and understand too that it is grandeur perverted, pitting itself against an enemy of its own making. Evil is real, 'has been from the beginning'; but Moby Dick is its agent only in Ahab's mind.

We cannot yet say just what the Ahab-Moby Dick anta- gonism represents—indeed Melville always leaves it more suggestive than precise. But clearly it images conflicting spiritual forces in the world and human life at large: man and Nature, human nobility and human malice, good and evil (strangely mingled).

The passage is also a study in morbid psychology: ob- serve how Ahab's mania develops secretly from 'sudden, passionate, corporal animosity'. The Ahab whom the crew see is quite different from the 'hidden self' revealed here. How does Melville emphasise the secret nature of Ahab's madness? Explain the point of the images in the final paragraph and say what they suggest about human nature.

Do you infer any general point about 'Life as we see it' in there being so much hidden from the crew?

Melville tells, basically, a simple story. Redburn sails to Liverpool and back; Ahab hunts Moby Dick who finally kills him. There is none of Dickens's complicated plot-making. Melville's narrative proceeds chronologically, picking out specific scenes and incidents on the way. These both convey the experience of living through the voyage and in different ways insinuate the wider meanings that Melville intends it to signify.

With the *Pequod* now well into the whaling-grounds and action imminent, the following passage describes a brief interval, peacefully suspended in time, of keenly responsive sympathy with the mood of the surroundings.

Scene and symbolism

II

Days, weeks passed, and under easy sail, the ivory *Pequod* had slowly swept across four several cruising-grounds; that off the Azores; off the Cape de Verdes; on the Plate (so called), being off the mouth of the Rio de la Plata; and the Carrol Ground, an unstaked, watery locality, southerly from St. Helena.

It was while gliding through these latter waters that one serene and moonlight night, when all the waves rolled by like scrolls of silver; and, by their soft, suffusing seethings, made what seemed a silvery silence, not a solitude: on such a silent night a silvery jet was seen far in advance of the white bubbles at the bow. Lit up by the moon, it looked celestial; seemed some plumed and glittering god uprising from the sea. Fedallah first descried this jet. For of these moonlight nights, it was his wont to mount to the main-masthead, and stand a look-out there, with the same precision as if it had been day. And yet, though herds of whales were seen by night, not one whaleman in a hundred would venture a lowering for them. You may think with what emotions, then, the seamen beheld this old Oriental perched aloft at such unusual hours; his turban and the moon, companions in one sky. But when, after spending his uniform interval there for several successive nights without uttering a single sound; when, after all this silence, his unearthly voice was heard announcing that silvery, moon-lit jet, every reclining mariner started to his feet as if some winged spirit had lighted in the rigging, and hailed the mortal crew. 'There she blows!' Had the trump of judgment blown, they could not have quivered more; yet still they felt no terror; rather pleasure. For though it was a most unwonted hour, yet so impressive was the cry, and so deliriously exciting, that almost every soul on board instinctively desired a lowering.

Walking the deck with quick, side-lunging strides, Ahab commanded the t'gallant sails and royals to be set, and every stunsail spread. The best man in the ship must take the helm. Then, with every mast-head manned, the piled-up craft rolled down before the wind. The strange, upheaving, lifting tendency of the taffrail breeze filling the hollows of so many sails, made the buoyant, hovering deck to feel like air beneath the feet; while still she rushed along, as if two antagonistic influences were struggling in her—one to mount direct to heaven, the other to drive yawingly to some horizontal goal. And had you watched Ahab's face that night, you would have thought that in him also two different things were warring. While his one live leg made lively echoes along the deck, every stroke of his dead limb sounded like a coffin-tap. On life and death this old man walked. But though the ship so swiftly sped, and though from every eye, like arrows, the eager glances shot, yet the silvery jet was no more seen that night. Every sailor swore he saw it once, but not a second time.

Moby Dick, ch. 51

The outstanding feature of the passage is its richly textured prose. Assonance and alliteration, emphatic rhythms, give it the quality of poetry. Indeed lines six-eleven fall easily into irregular verse-lines. The third paragraph reverses the mood of the second: how does Melville bring this about, particularly by the contrasting rhythm and structure of their sentences?

Natural harmony disrupted by human intrusion; the 'antagonistic influences' (how do you interpret these?) in the *Pequod*'s voyage; the coincidence of life and death in Ahab: these ideas, fundamental to the novel, emerge from and are integrated with the scene itself, and the way in which its qualities are expressed. Consequently there is no discontinuity between concrete scene and abstract ideas. The next excerpt makes rather similar use of a scene, though it draws a fuller and more explicit analogy.

12

It was a cloudy, sultry afternoon; the seamen were lazily lounging about the decks, or vacantly gazing over into the lead-colored waters. Queequeg and I were mildly employed weaving what is called a sword-mat, for an additional lashing to our boat. So still and subdued and yet somehow preluding was all the scene, and such an incantation of revery lurked in the air, that each silent sailor seemed resolved into his own invisible self.

I was the attendant or page of Queequeg, while busy at the mat. As I kept passing and repassing the filling or woof of marline between the long yarns of the warp, using my own hand for the shuttle, and as Queequeg, standing sideways, ever and anon slid his heavy oaken sword between the threads, and idly looking off upon the water, carelessly and unthinkingly drove home every yarn: I say so strange a dreaminess did there then reign all over the ship and all over the sea, only broken by the intermitting dull sound of the sword, that it seemed as if this were the Loom of Time, and I myself were a shuttle mechanically weaving and weaving away at the Fates. There lay the fixed threads of the warp subject to but one single, ever returning, un-changing vibration, and that vibration merely enough to admit of the crosswise interblending of other threads with its own. This warp seemed necessity; and here, thought I, with my own hand I ply my own shuttle and weave my own destiny into these unalterable threads. Meantime, Queequeg's impulsive, indifferent sword, sometimes hitting the woof slantingly, or crookedly, or strongly, or weakly, as the case might be; and by this difference in the conclud-ing blow producing a corresponding contrast in the final aspect of the completed fabric; this savage's sword, thought I, which thus finally shapes and fashions both warp and woof; this easy, indifferent sword must be chance—aye, chance, free will, and necessity—no wise incompatible—all interweavingly working together. The straight warp of necessity, not to be swerved from its ultimate course—its every alternating vibration, indeed, only tending to that; freewill still free to ply her shuttle between given threads; and chance, though restrained in its play within the right lines of necessity, and sideways in its motions directed by free will, though thus prescribed to by both, chance by turns rules either, and has the last featuring blow at events.

Moby Dick, ch. 47

How would you describe the mood of this scene and how does Melville establish it?

Melville's analogy takes up the theological riddles of free will, predestination (necessity) and chance in the work-ing out of human destiny: if God has determined the future, how can man have free will; if man is free to choose, how can God 'know' the future? Yet how can an omniscient God *not* know the future? How does the ana-logy interpret these paradoxes? Within what broader framework does it place the *Pequod*'s voyage?

The symbolism of nature

The remaining extracts form a sequence. In the first,

Stubb, second mate, kills a whale in the Indian Ocean, nearing Java.

13

'Haul in—haul in!' cried Stubb to the bowsman! and, facing round towards the whale, all hands began pulling the boat up to him, while yet the boat was being towed on. Soon ranging up by his flank, Stubb, firmly planting his knee in the clumsy cleat, darted dart after dart into the flying fish; at the word of command, the boat alternately sterning out of the way of the whale's horrible wallow, and then ranging up for another fling.

The red tide now poured from all sides of the monster like brooks down a hill. His tormented body rolled not in brine but in blood, which bubbled and seethed for furlongs behind in their wake. The slanting sun playing upon this crimson pond in the sea, sent back its reflection into every face, so that they all glowed to each other like red men. And all the while, jet after jet of white smoke was agonizingly shot from the spiracle of the whale, and vehement puff after puff from the mouth of the excited headsman; as at every dart, hauling in upon his crooked lance (by the line attached to it), Stubb straightened it again and again by a few rapid blows against the gunwale, then again and again sent it into the whale.

'Pull up—pull up!' he now cried to the bowsman, as the waning whale relaxed in his wrath. 'Pull up!—close to!' and the boat ranged along the fish's flank. When reaching far over the bow, Stubb slowly churned his long sharp lance into the fish, and kept it there, carefully churning and churning, as if cautiously seeking to feel after some gold watch that the whale might have swallowed, and which he was fearful of breaking ere he could hook it out. But that gold watch he sought was the innermost life of the fish. And now it is struck; for, starting from his trance into that unspeakable thing called his 'flurry', the monster horribly wallowed in his blood, overwrapped himself in

43

impenetrable, mad, boiling spray, so that the imperilled craft, instantly dropping astern, had much ado blindly to struggle out from that phrensied twilight into the clear air of the day.

And now abating in his flurry, the whale once more rolled out into view; surging from side to side; spasmodically dilating and contracting his spout-hole, with sharp, cracking, agonized respirations. At last, gush after gush of clotted red gore, as if it had been the purple lees of red wine, shot into the frighted air; and falling back again, ran dripping down his motionless flanks into the sea. His heart had burst!

'He's dead, Mr. Stubb,' said Daggoo.

'Yes; both pipes smoked out!' and withdrawing his own from his mouth, Stubb scattered the dead ashes over the water; and, for a moment, stood thoughtfully eyeing the vast corpse he had made.

Moby Dick, ch. 61

Melville portrays the act of dying in violent, convulsive motion. Both verbs and nouns—'sterning', 'wallow', 'ranging', 'fling'—maintain the sense of agonised commotion. The colour of blood saturates the whole scene. Show how the verbal detail produces the total effect.

This scene of slaughter makes man a part of predatory Nature, violent, destructive. The next extract reinforces the mood of death and extends this view of nature—'insatiate sharks', 'rapacious fowls', 'murderous din'—paradoxically set in a mild and lovely scene.

14

'Haul in the chains! Let the carcase go astern!' The vast tackles have now done their duty. The peeled white body of the beheaded whale flashes like a marble sepulchre; though changed in hue, it has not perceptibly lost anything in bulk. It is still colossal. Slowly it floats more and more

away, the water round it torn and splashed by the insatiate
sharks, and the air above vexed with rapacious flights of
screaming fowls, whose beaks are like so many insulting
poniards in the whale. The vast white headless phantom
floats further and further from the ship, and every rod that
it so floats, what seem square roods of sharks and cubic
roods of fowls, augment the murderous din. For hours and
hours from the almost stationary ship that hideous sight is
seen. Beneath the unclouded and mild azure sky, upon the
fair face of the pleasant sea, wafted by the joyous breezes,
the great mass of death floats on and on, till lost in infinite
perspectives.

There's a most doleful and most mocking funeral! The
sea-vultures all in pious mourning, the air-sharks all punc-
tiliously in black or speckled. In life but few of them would
have helped the whale, I ween, if peradventure he had
needed it; but upon the banquet of his funeral they most
piously do pounce. Oh, horrible vulturism of earth! from
which not the mightiest whale is free . . .

Moby Dick, ch. 69

The *Pequod*'s whale being decapitated and the body
stripped, the head was hoisted against the ship's side—
about half way out of the sea, so that it might yet in great
part be buoyed up by its native element. And there with
the strained craft steeply leaning over it, by reason of
the enormous downward drag from the lower mast-head,
and every yard-arm on that side projecting like a crane over
the waves; there, that blood-dripping head hung to the
Pequod's waist like the giant Holofernes's[4] from the girdle
of Judith.

When this last task was accomplished it was noon, and
the seamen went below to their dinner. Silence reigned over
the before tumultuous but now deserted deck. An intense
copper calm, like a universal yellow lotus, was more and
more unfolding its noiseless measureless leaves upon the
sea.

A short space elapsed, and up into this noiselessness came

[4] Nebuchadnezzar's general, killed by Judith (*Judith*, iv, I, etc.)

45

Ahab alone from his cabin. Taking a few turns on the quarter-deck, he paused to gaze over the side, then slowly getting into the main-chains he took Stubb's long spade—still remaining there after the whale's decapitation—and striking it into the lower part of the half-suspended mass, placed its other end crutch-wise under one arm, and so stood leaning over with eyes attentively fixed on this head.

It was a black and hooded head; and hanging there in the midst of so intense a calm, it seemed the Sphynx's in the desert. 'Speak thou vast and venerable head,' muttered Ahab, 'which, though ungarnished with a beard, yet here and there lookest hoary with mosses; speak, mighty head, and tell us the secret thing that is in thee. Of all divers thou hast dived the deepest. That head upon which the upper sun now gleams, has moved amid this world's foundations. Where unrecorded names and navies rust, and untold hopes and anchors rot; where in her murderous hold this frigate earth is ballasted with bones of millions of the drowned; there, in that awful water-land, there was thy most familiar home. Thou hast been where bell or diver never went; hast slept by many a sailor's side, where sleepless mothers would give their lives to lay them down. Thou saw'st the locked lovers when leaping from their flaming ship; heart to heart they sank beneath the exulting wave; true to each other, when heaven seemed false to them. Thou saw'st the murdered mate when tossed by pirates from the midnight deck; for hours he fell into the deeper midnight of the insatiate maw; and his murderers still sailed on unharmed—while swift lightnings shivered the neighboring ship that would have borne a righteous husband to outstretched, longing arms. O head! thou hast seen enough to split the planets and make an infidel of Abraham, and not one syllable is thine!'

'Sail ho!' cried a triumphant voice from the main-mast-head.

'Aye? Well, now, that's cheering,' cried Ahab, suddenly erecting himself, while whole thunder-clouds swept aside from his brow. 'That lively cry upon this deadly calm might almost convert a better man.—Where away?'

'Three points on the starboard bow, sir, and bringing down her breeze to us!'

'Better and better, man. Would now St. Paul would come along that way, and to my breezelessness bring his breeze! O Nature, and O soul of man! how far beyond all utterance are your linked analogies! not the smallest atom stirs or lives on matter, but has its cunning duplicate in mind.'

Moby Dick, ch. 70

When Ahab enters and soliloquises on the dead whale's head, he sees it as an emblem of all the suffering and loss wreaked by the sea. The still calm belies the ocean's true nature; the vast corpse and the savagery which has produced it more accurately reflect the reality of life. What 'cunning duplicates' between matter and mind does the passage suggest to you?

Shortly afterwards, nearer Java, the *Pequod* comes upon another scene, which questions this estimate of nature's essential savagery. Nursing whales play with their young.

15

But far beneath this wondrous world upon the surface, another and still stranger world met our eyes as we gazed over the side. For, suspended in those watery vaults, floated the forms of the nursing mothers of the whales, and those that by their enormous girth seemed shortly to become mothers. The lake, as I have hinted, was to a considerable depth exceedingly transparent; and as human infants while suckling will calmly and fixedly gaze away from the breast, as if leading two different lives at the time; and while yet drawing mortal nourishment, be still spiritually feasting upon some unearthly reminiscence;—even so did the young of these whales seem looking up towards us, but not at us, as if we were but a bit of Gulf-weed in their new-born sight. Floating on their sides, the mothers also seemed

47

quietly eyeing us. One of these little infants, that from certain queer tokens seemed hardly a day old, might have measured some fourteen feet in length, and some six feet in girth. He was a little frisky; though as yet his body seemed scarce yet recovered from that irksome position it had so lately occupied in the maternal reticule; where, tail to head, and all ready for the final spring, the unborn whale lies bent like a Tartar's bow. The delicate side-fins, and the palms of his flukes, still freshly retained the plaited crumpled appearance of a baby's ears newly arrived from foreign parts.

'Line! line!' cried Queequeg, looking over the gunwale; 'him fast! him fast—Who line him! Who struck?—Two whale; one big, one little!'

'What ails ye, man?' cried Starbuck.

'Look-e here,' said Queequeg pointing down.

As when the stricken whale, that from the tub has reeled out hundreds of fathoms of rope; as, after deep sounding, he floats up again, and shows the slackened curling line buoyantly rising and spiralling towards the air; so now, Starbuck saw long coils of the umbilical cord of Madame Leviathan, by which the young cub seemed still tethered to its dam. Not seldom in the rapid vicissitudes of the chase, this natural line, with the maternal end loose, becomes entangled with the hempen one, so that the cub is thereby trapped. Some of the subtlest secrets of the seas seemed divulged to us in this enchanted pond. We saw young Leviathan amours in the deep.

And thus, though surrounded by circle upon circle of consternations and affrights, did these inscrutable creatures at the centre freely and fearlessly indulge in all peaceful concernments; yea, serenely revelled in dalliance and delight. But even so, amid the tornadoed Atlantic of my being, do I myself still for ever centrally disport in mute calm; and while ponderous planets of unwaning woe revolve round me, deep down and deep inland there I still bathe me in eternal mildness of joy.

Moby Dick, ch. 87

What is the contrasting mood of this passage? How is it conveyed?

The sequence as a whole presents an equivocal view of Nature, and through this conflicting forces in man and the world he inhabits. In Nature seeming incompatibles go side by side. It is destructive and creative both, mild and tempestuous; prey and hunter are one. Similarly man: within his distraught being Ishmael feels a still centre, like an inland haven from the dangerous ocean. Another short passage expands this metaphor: the contrasts within Nature and within the ocean must be set alongside a contrast between sea and land. The excerpt precedes the foregoing passages, but can equally be a sequel to them.

16

Consider the subtleness of the sea; how its most dreaded creatures glide under water, unapparent for the most part, and treacherously hidden beneath the loveliest tints of azure. Consider also the devilish brilliance and beauty of many of its most remorseless tribes, as the dainty embellished shape of many species of sharks. Consider, once more, the universal cannibalism of the sea; all whose creatures prey upon each other, carrying on eternal war since the world began.

Consider all this; and then turn to this green, gentle, and most docile earth; consider them both, the sea and the land; and do you not find a strange analogy to something in yourself? For as this appalling ocean surrounds the verdant land, so in the soul of man there lies one insular Tahiti, full of peace and joy, but encompassed by all the horrors of the half known life. God keep thee! Push not off from that isle, thou canst never return!

Moby Dick, ch. 58

The 'insular Tahiti' is a compressed version of Melville's Eden-like Nukuheva, a refuge from the destructive sea. Yet to cast off from the island, though perilous, has a heroic

49

grandeur, a challenge to human aspiration, just as Ahab and his voyage have such grandeur, though misguided and doomed to ruin. The land/sea antithesis is no less cryptic than Melville's equivocal Nature. In a different set of images, our final extract further qualifies Melville's statement. Ishmael is on watch at night with the try-works, the forges where the blubber is reduced to oil, in operation.

17

But that night, in particular, a strange (and ever since inexplicable) thing occurred to me. Starting from a brief standing sleep, I was horribly conscious of something fatally wrong. The jaw-bone tiller smote my side, which leaned against it; in my ears was the low hum of sails, just beginning to shake in the wind; I thought my eyes were open; I was half conscious of putting my fingers to the lids and mechanically stretching them still further apart. But, spite of all this, I could see no compass before me to steer by; though it seemed but a minute since I had been watching the card, by the steady binnacle lamp illuminating it. Nothing seemed before me but a jet gloom, now and then made ghastly by flashes of redness. Uppermost was the impression, that whatever swift, rushing thing I stood on was not so much bound to any haven ahead as rushing from all havens astern. A stark, bewildered feeling, as of death, came over me. Convulsively my hands grasped the tiller, but with the crazy conceit that the tiller was, somehow, in some enchanted way, inverted. My God! what is the matter with me? thought I. Lo! in my brief sleep I had turned myself about, and was fronting the ship's stern, with my back to her prow and the compass. In an instant I faced back, just in time to prevent the vessel from flying up into the wind, and very probably capsizing her. How glad and how grateful the relief from this unnatural hallucination of the night, and the fatal contingency of being brought by the lee!

Look not too long in the face of the fire, O man! Never dream with thy hand on the helm! Turn not thy back to the compass; accept the first hint of the hitching tiller; believe not the artificial fire, when its redness makes all things look ghastly. To-morrow, in the natural sun, the skies will be bright; those who glared like devils in the forking flames, the morn will show in far other, at least gentler, relief; the glorious, golden, glad sun, the only true lamp—all others but liars!

Nevertheless the sun hides not Virginia's Dismal Swamp, nor Rome's accursed Campagna, nor wide Sahara, nor all the millions of miles of desert and of griefs beneath the moon. The sun hides not the ocean, which is the dark side of this earth, and which is two-thirds of this earth. So, therefore, that mortal man who hath more of joy than sorrow in him, that mortal man cannot be true—not true, or undeveloped. With books the same. The truest of all men was the Man of Sorrows, and the truest of all books is Solomon's, and Ecclesiastes is the fine hammered steel of woe. 'All is vanity.' ALL. This wilful world hath not got hold of unchristian Solomon's wisdom yet. But he who dodges hospitals and jails, and walks fast crossing grave-yards, and would rather talk of operas than hell; calls Cowper, Young, Pascal, Rousseau, poor devils all of sick men; and throughout a care-free lifetime swears by Rabelais as passing wise, and therefore jolly;—not that man is fitted to sit down on tomb-stones, and break the green damp mould with unfathomably wondrous Solomon.

But even Solomon, he says, 'the man that wandereth out of the way of understanding shall remain' (*i.e.* even while living) 'in the congregation of the dead.' Give not thyself up, then, to fire, lest it invert thee, deaden thee; as for the time it did me. There is a wisdom that is woe; but there is a woe that is madness. And there is a Catskill eagle in some souls than can alike dive down into the blackest gorges, and soar out of them again and become invisible in the sunny spaces. And even if he for ever flies within the gorge, that gorge is in the mountains; so that even in his

lowest swoop the mountain eagle is still higher than other
birds upon the plain, even though they soar.

Moby Dick, ch. 96

Explain carefully the sequence of thought which leads
Melville from the try-works to the image of the eagle.

Most of the images for the evil, oppressive qualities of
life come from inland scenes, urban and rural—no longer
the haven-like Tahiti. But Melville does not intend these
as an exclusive view of life: 'sunny spaces' balances 'blackest gorges'; the eagle's soaring balances its plunges.

Moby Dick's meanings are multiple and intended to present, not solve, the human situation. They are insusceptible
of neat summary. But a key to the above passage—and perhaps to *Moby Dick* itself—is the sentence, 'There is a wisdom that is woe; but there is a woe that is madness.'
Wisdom demands recognition, perhaps even experience, of
life's afflictions. But it is madness to permit them entire
possession of the mind.

The novel's passing scenes present the paradoxical variety
in man and Nature both, the emphasis sombre, certainly
not suggesting a universe ruled by a benevolent God, but
not despairing. Ending in ruin with Moby Dick destroying
the *Pequod* and its crew, it is a tragedy, almost Shakes-
pearean, of greatness wasted. Yet not entirely wasted.
Ishmael survives to reach some sort of salvation; and to
tell his tale. How would you now interpret the final
sequence of extracts?

Ishmael tells most of the story. But as a 'narrative
medium' he is inconsistent. At times he disappears entirely,
replaced by dialogue set out as in a play, soliloquies from
Ahab and others, interpolated stories from ships the
Pequod meets, long documentary passages on the history
and techniques of whaling. At times Ishmael passes on information which, realistically, he could not possibly know:

52

Ahab's thoughts and private actions, for example.

Melville was a lone experimenter not much troubled by consistency. He wanted both the immediacy of passages like the last one, with Ishmael at the centre, and the greater freedom of omniscient narration. He therefore switched manners as he chose. Look through all the extracts given for examples of this inconsistency. Generally, how do you respond to Melville's treatment of the voyage and its incidents as symbolising man's spiritual nature and his place in the universe?

'Bartleby', 'Benito Cereno': social man and the outcast

The story and the meaning: techniques of indirect commentary

Moby Dick did not sell; nor its successor, *Pierre*, a tortured story of the artist alienated from society. While of great interest to Melville scholars, it is on the outskirts of his achievement.

In his remaining years, which never repeated his early success, Melville was often depressed and ill. But he never ceased to write; now singlemindedly pursuing his own way, he no longer sought popular favour. In his two best short stories, compassionate, probing studies of psychological collapse, critics have seen reflected Melville's own relationship with the public—as in Bartleby's silences, his refusal to do what is expected of him. But whatever undercurrents from his own life may stir in them, they reach beyond merely personal relevance.

The narrator of 'Bartleby' is a lawyer who has hired Bartleby as a scrivener, with the task of endlessly copying legal documents. Bartleby grows increasingly more aloof and remote from life. Increasingly, without explanation, he 'prefers not to' do his job. In desperation, the lawyer quits his office. Refusing to leave it, Bartleby is jailed.

Being under no disgraceful charge, and quite serene and harmless in all his ways, they had permitted him freely to wander about the prison, and, especially, in the enclosed grass-platted yards thereof. And so I found him there, standing all alone in the quietest of the yards, his face towards a high wall, while all around, from the narrow slits of the jail windows, I thought I saw peering out upon him the eyes of murderers and thieves.

'Bartleby!'

'I know you,' he said, without looking round—'and I want nothing to say to you.'

'It was not I that brought you here, Bartleby,' said I, keenly pained at his implied suspicion. 'And to you, this should not be so vile a place. Nothing reproachful attaches to you by being here. And see, it is not so sad a place as one might think. Look, there is the sky, and here is the grass.'

'I know where I am,' he replied, but would say nothing more, and so I left him.

As I entered the corridor again, a broad meat-like man, in an apron, accosted me, and, jerking his thumb over his shoulder, said—'Is that your friend?'

'Yes.'

'Does he want to starve? If he does, let him live on the prison fare, that's all.'

'Who are you?' asked I, not knowing what to make of such an unofficially speaking person in such a place.

'I am the grub-man. Such gentlemen as have friends here, hire me to provide them with something good to eat.'

'Is this so?' said I, turning to the turnkey.

He said it was.

'Well, then,' said I, slipping some silver into the grub-man's hands (for so they called him), 'I want you to give particular attention to my friend there; let him have the best dinner you can get. And you must be as polite to him as possible.'

55

'Introduce me, will you?' said the grub-man, looking at me with an expression which seemed to say he was all impatience for an opportunity to give a specimen of his breeding.

Thinking it would prove of benefit to the scrivener, I acquiesced; and, asking the grub-man his name, went up with him to Bartleby.

'Bartleby, this is a friend; you will find him very useful to you.'

'Your sarvant, sir, your sarvant,' said the grub-man, making a low salutation behind his apron. 'Hope you find it pleasant here, sir; nice grounds—cool apartments—hope you'll stay with us sometime—try to make it agreeable. What will you have for dinner to-day?'

'I prefer not to dine to-day,' said Bartleby, turning away. 'It would disagree with me; I am unused to dinners.' So saying, he slowly moved to the other side of the enclosure, and took up a position fronting the dead-wall.

'How's this?' said the grub-man, addressing me with a stare of astonishment. 'He's odd, ain't he?'

'I think he is a little deranged,' said I sadly.

'Deranged? deranged is it? Well, now, upon my word, I thought that friend of yourn was a gentleman forger; they are always pale and genteel-like, them forgers. I can't help pity 'em—can't help it, sir. Did you know Monroe Edwards?' he added touchingly, and paused. Then, laying his hand piteously on my shoulder, sighed, 'he died of consumption at Sing-Sing. So you weren't acquainted with Monroe?'

'No, I was never socially acquainted with any forgers. But I cannot stop longer. Look to my friend yonder. You will not lose by it. I will see you again.'

Some few days after this, I again obtained admission to the Tombs,[1] and went through the corridors in quest of Bartleby; but without finding him.

___

[1] The name of the New York prison to which Bartleby had been committed.

'I saw him coming from his cell not long ago,' said a turnkey, 'may be he's gone to loiter in the yards.'

So I went in that direction.

'Are you looking for the silent man?' said another turnkey, passing me. 'Yonder he lies—sleeping in the yard there. 'Tis not twenty minutes since I saw him lie down.'

The yard was entirely quiet. It was not accessible to the common prisoners. The surrounding walls, of amazing thickness, kept off all sounds behind them. The Egyptian character of the masonry weighed upon me with its gloom. But a soft imprisoned turf grew under foot. The heart of the eternal pyramids, it seemed, wherein, by some strange magic, through the clefts, grass-seed, dropped by birds, had sprung.

Strangely huddled at the base of the wall, his knees drawn up, and lying on his side, his head touching the cold stones, I saw the wasted Bartleby. But nothing stirred. I paused; then went close up to him; stooped over, and saw that his dim eyes were open; otherwise he seemed profoundly sleeping. Something prompted me to touch him. I felt his hand, when a tingling shiver ran up my arm and down my spine to my feet.

The round face of the grub-man peered upon me now. 'His dinner is ready. Won't he dine to-day, either? Or does he live without dining?'

'Lives without dining,' said I, and closed the eyes.

'Eh!—He's asleep, ain't he?'

'With kings and counsellors,' murmured I.

There would seem little need for proceeding further in this history. Imagination will readily supply the meagre recital of poor Bartleby's interment. But, ere parting with the reader, let me say, that if this little narrative has sufficiently interested him, to awaken curiosity as to who Bartleby was, and what manner of life he led prior to the present narrator's making his acquaintance, I can only reply, that in such curiosity I fully share, but am wholly unable to gratify it. Yet here I hardly know whether I should divulge one little item of rumor, which came to my ear a few months after the scrivener's decease. Upon what basis it rested I could never ascertain; and hence, how true it is I cannot now tell. But, inasmuch as this vague report has not been without a certain suggestive interest to me, however sad, it may prove the same with some others; and so I will briefly mention it. The report was this: that Bartleby had been a subordinate clerk in the Dead Letter Office at Washington, from which he had been suddenly removed by a change in the administration. When I think over this rumor, hardly can I express the emotions which seize me. Dead letters! does it not sound like dead men? Conceive a man by nature and misfortune prone to a pallid hopelessness, can any business seem more fitted to heighten it than that of continually handling these dead letters, and assorting them for the flames? For by the cart-load they are annually burned. Sometimes from out the folded paper the pale clerk takes a ring—the finger it was meant for, perhaps, moulders in the grave; a bank-note sent in swiftest charity—he whom it would relieve, nor eats nor hungers any more; pardon for those who died despairing; hope for those who died unhoping; good tidings for those who died stifled by unrelieved calamities. On errands of life, these letters speed to death.

Ah, Bartleby! Ah, humanity!

Bartleby the Scrivener

Bartleby and the narrator are worlds apart, despite the lawyer's sympathy. The lawyer's professional world is respectable, practical. From this Bartleby has withdrawn into some psychological bolthole, finally into death. He is a refugee from life, which offers him as refuge only a prison. Melville does not make this explicit. Bartleby is presented indirectly as a casualty of modern society.

The following phrases suggest Bartleby's attitude to life: 'His face towards a high wall', 'fronting the dead wall', 'huddled at the base of the wall'. By what other indirect means does Melville indicate the significance of Bartleby and his situation? What do you take that significance to be? Would the ending lose anything without the grub-man or without its final section?

At the beginning of 'Benito Cereno' Amasa Delano, captain of an American sealer, sees a distressed ship, the *San Dominick*.

19

The morning was one peculiar to that coast.[2] Everything was mute and calm; everything gray. The sea, though undulated into long roods of swells, seemed fixed, and was sleeked at the surface like waved lead that has cooled and set in the smelter's mold. The sky seemed a gray surtout. Flights of troubled gray fowl, kith and kin with flights of troubled gray vapors among which they were mixed, skimmed low and fitfully over the waters, as swallows over meadows before storms. Shadows present, foreshadowing deeper shadows to come.

To Captain Delano's surprise, the stranger, viewed through the glass, showed no colors; though to do so upon entering a haven, however uninhabited in its shores, where but a single other ship might be lying, was the custom among peaceful seamen of all nations. Considering the lawlessness and loneliness of the spot, and the sort of stories, at that day, associated with those seas, Captain Delano's surprise might have deepened into some uneasiness had he not been a person of a singularly undistrustful good nature, not liable, except on extraordinary and repeated incentives, and hardly then, to indulge in personal alarms, any way involving the imputation of malign evil in man. Whether, in view of what humanity is capable, such a trait implies, along with a benevolent heart, more

[2] Of Chile.

than ordinary quickness and accuracy of intellectual perception, may be left to the wise to determine.

But whatever misgivings might have obtruded on first seeing the stranger, would almost, in any seaman's mind, have been dissipated by observing that the ship, in navigating into the harbor was drawing too near the land; a sunken reef making out off her bow. This seemed to prove her a stranger, indeed, not only to the sealer, but the island; consequently, she could be no wonted freebooter on that ocean. With no small interest, Captain Delano continued to watch her—a proceeding not much facilitated by the vapors partly mantling the hull, through which the far matin light from her cabin streamed equivocally enough; much like the sun—by this time hemisphered on the rim of the horizon, and, apparently, in company with the strange ship entering the harbor—which, wimpled by the same low, creeping clouds, showed not unlike a Lima *intriguante*'s one sinister eye peering across the Plaza from the Indian loop-hole of her dusk *saya-y-manta*.

It might have been but a deception of the vapors, but the longer the stranger was watched the more singular appeared her manoeuvres. Ere long it seemed hard to decide whether she meant to come in or no—what she wanted, or what she was about. The wind, which had breezed up a little during the night, was now extremely light and baffling, which the more increased the apparent uncertainty of her movements. . . .

Upon gaining a less remote view, the ship, when made signally visible on the verge of the leaden-hued swells, with the shreds of fog here and there raggedly furring her, appeared like a white-washed monastery after a thunderstorm, seen perched upon some dun cliff among the Pyrenees. But it was no purely fanciful resemblance which now, for a moment, almost led Captain Delano to think that nothing less than a shipload of monks was before him. Peering over the bulwarks were what really seemed, in the hazy distance, throngs of dark cowls; while, fitfully revealed through the open port-holes, other dark moving figures were dimly descried, as of Black Friars pacing the cloisters.

Upon a still nigher approach, this appearance was modified, and the true character of the vessel was plain—a Spanish merchantman of the first class, carrying negro slaves, amongst other valuable freight, from one colonial port to another. A very large, and, in its time, a very fine vessel, such as in those days were at intervals encountered along that main; sometimes superseded Acapulco treasure-ships, or retired frigates of the Spanish king's navy, which, like superannuated Italian palaces, still, under a decline of masters, preserved signs of former state.

As the whale-boat drew more and more nigh, the cause of the peculiar pipe-clayed aspect of the stranger was seen in the slovenly neglect pervading her. The spars, ropes, and great part of the bulwarks, looked woolly, from long un-acquaintance with the scraper, tar, and the brush. Her keel seemed laid, her ribs put together, and she launched, from Ezekiel's Valley of Dry Bones.

Benito Cereno

We follow events through what Delano sees and thinks. But Melville also discreetly colours Delano's impressions to define mood and atmosphere. So, while we share his gradual discoveries, we are more aware of the situation's menace, and recognise implications to which he is blind. The phrase, for example, 'Shadows present, foreshadowing deeper shadows to come' is not Delano's premonition but a comment from Melville, though it avoids making us conscious of his presence, as author, guiding us.

Delano's character is important to the story. What do you learn of it? How would it affect his assessment of events? How much of the atmosphere of these paragraphs is apparent to Delano, how much 'fed in' by Melville, and by what means?—Consider the description of the mist-shrouded ship: it is Melville who supplies 'not unlike a Lima intriguante's one *sinister* eye'.

Delano boards the *San Dominick*. Its captain, Benito Cereno, tells him of storms and fever which have brought the ship to grief. Various circumstances strike even the credulous Delano as odd: disproportionate losses among the Spanish seamen; the undisciplined, threatening attitude of the negroes; Cereno's alternately overwrought and apathetic moods, his dependence on his negro servant, Babo.

20

Here, passing from one suspicious thing to another, his mind revolved the strange questions put to him concerning his ship.[3]

By a curious coincidence, as each point was recalled, the black wizards of Ashantee[4] would strike up with their hatchets, as in ominous comment on the white stranger's thoughts. Pressed by such enigmas and portents, it would have been almost against nature, had not, even into the least distrustful heart, some ugly misgivings obtruded.

Observing the ship, now helplessly fallen into a current, with enchanted sails, drifting with increased rapidity seaward; and noting that from a lately intercepted projection of the land, the sealer was hidden, the stout mariner began to quake at thoughts which he barely durst confess to himself. Above all, he began to feel a ghostly dread of Don Benito. And yet, when he roused himself, dilated his chest, felt himself strong on his legs, and coolly considered it—what did all these phantoms amount to?

Had the Spaniard any sinister scheme, it must have reference not so much to him (Captain Delano) as to his ship (the *Bachelor's Delight*). Hence the present drifting away of the one ship from the other, instead of favoring any such possible scheme, was, for the time, at least, opposed to it. Clearly any suspicion, combining such contradictions, must need be delusive. Besides, was it not absurd to think of a

[3] Cereno had asked the number of its crew and if it was armed.
[4] A territory in the north of present-day Ghana.

vessel in distress—a vessel by sickness almost dismanned of her crew—a vessel whose inmates were parched for water—was it not a thousand times absurd that such a craft should, at present, be of a piratical character; or her commander, either for himself or those under him, cherish any desire but for speedy relief and refreshment? But then, might not general distress, and thirst in particular, be affected? And might not that same undiminished Spanish crew, alleged to have perished off to a remnant, be at that very moment lurking in the hold? . . .

He recalled the Spaniard's manner while telling his story. There was a gloomy hesitancy and subterfuge about it. It was just the manner of one making up his tale for evil purposes, as he goes. But if that story was not true, what was the truth? That the ship had unlawfully come into the Spaniard's possession? But in many of its details, especially in reference to the more calamitous parts, such as the fatalities among the seamen, the consequent prolonged beating about, the past sufferings from obstinate calms, and still continued suffering from thirst; in all these points, as well as others, Don Benito's story had corroborated not only the wailing ejaculations of the indiscriminate multitude, white and black, but likewise—what seemed impossible to be counterfeit—by the very expression and play of every human feature, which Captain Delano saw. If Don Benito's story was, throughout, an invention, then every soul on board, down to the youngest negress, was his carefully drilled recruit in the plot: an incredible inference. And yet, if there was ground for mistrusting his veracity, that inference was a legitimate one.

But those questions of the Spaniard. There, indeed, one might pause. Did they not seem put with much the same object with which the burglar or assassin, by day-time, reconnoitres the walls of a house? But, with ill purposes, to solicit such information openly of the chief person endangered, and so, in effect, setting him on his guard; how unlikely a procedure was that. Absurd, then, to suppose that those questions had been prompted by evil designs.

63

Thus, the same conduct, which, in this instance, had raised the alarm, served to dispel it. In short, scarce any suspicion or uneasiness, however apparently reasonable at the time, which was not now, with equal apparent reason, dismissed.

At last he began to laugh at his former forebodings; and laugh at the strange ship for, in its aspect, someway siding with them, as it were; and laugh, too, at the odd-looking blacks, particularly those old scissors-grinders, the Ashantees; and those bed-ridden old knitting women, the oakumpickets; and almost at the dark Spaniard himself, the central hobgoblin of all.

Benito Cereno

Here the enigmatic situation assails the commonsense Delano with a flurry of doubts and questions. We follow the rapid succession of thoughts, the various possible and conflicting explanations of what he has observed. His suspicions turn entirely on *physical* danger; and finally he persuades himself that the only explanation that will account for all appearances is an innocent one.

It emerges that the negroes, at Babo's instigation, had seized the ship and murdered most of the crew; and with Delano's arrival improvised the deception that Cereno was still in command. Delano's crew subdue the negroes and capture the ship, disclosing on its shrouded prow, as a figurehead, the skeleton of Cereno's best friend, and the sardonic chalked legend, *Seguid vuestre jefe*: follow your leader.

21

'Wide indeed,' said Don Benito sadly; 'you were with me all day; stood with me, sat with me, talked with me, looked at me, drank with me; and yet, your last act was to clutch for a monster, not only an innocent man, but the most pitiable of all men. To such a degree may malign machinations and deceptions impose. So far may even the best man err, in judging the conduct of one with the recesses of whose condition he is not acquainted. But you were forced to it; and you were in time undeceived. Would that, in both respects, it was so ever, and with all men.'

'You generalize, Don Benito; and mournfully enough. But the past is passed; why moralize upon it? Forget it. See, yon bright sun has forgotten it all, and the blue sea, and the blue sky; these have turned over new leaves.'

'Because they have no memory,' he dejectedly replied; 'because they are not human.'

'But these mild Trades that now fan your cheek, do they not come with a human-like healing to you? Warm friends, steadfast friends are the Trades.'

'With their steadfastness they but waft me to my tomb, Señor,' was the foreboding response.

'You are saved,' cried Captain Delano, more and more astonished and pained; 'you are saved: what has cast such a shadow upon you?'

'The negro.'

There was silence, while the moody man sat, slowly and unconsciously gathering his mantle about him, as if it were a pall.

There was no more conversation that day.

But if the Spaniard's melancholy sometimes ended in muteness upon topics like the above, there were others upon which he never spoke at all; on which, indeed, all his old reserves were piled. Pass over the worst, and, only to elucidate, let an item or two of these be cited. The dress, so precise and costly, worn by him on the day whose events have been narrated, had not willingly been put on. And that silver-mounted sword, apparent symbol of despotic command, was not, indeed, a sword, but the ghost of one. The scabbard, artificially stiffened, was empty.

As for the black—whose brain, not body, had schemed and led the revolt, with the plot—his slight frame, inadequate to that which it held, had at once yielded to the superior muscular strength of his captor, in the boat. Seeing all was over, he uttered no sound, and could not be forced to. His aspect seemed to say, since I cannot do deeds, I will not speak words. Put in irons in the hold, with the rest, he was carried to Lima. During the passage, Don Benito did not visit him. Nor then, nor at any time after, would he look at him. Before the tribunal he refused. When pressed by the judges he fainted. On the testimony of the sailors alone rested the legal identity of Babo.

Some months after, dragged to the gibbet at the tail of a mule, the black met his voiceless end. The body was burned to ashes; but for many days, the head, that hive of subtlety, fixed on a pole in the Plaza, met, unabashed, the gaze of the whites; and across the Plaza looked towards St. Bartholomew's church, in whose vaults slept then, as now, the recovered bones of Aranda: and across the Rimac bridge looked towards the monastery, on Mount Agonia without; where, three months after being dismissed by the court, Benito Cereno, borne on the bier, did, indeed, follow his leader.

Benito Cereno

Benito Cereno is the 'failure' here. Danger behind him, Delano renews his bland confidence, all misgivings forgotten—'the past is passed; why moralise upon it?' But Cereno's will has totally disintegrated, even the will to live, the cause being, he says, 'The negro.' There is more to it than just Babo's cunning and ruthlessness. He has completely imposed himself on Cereno, consuming his personality with the weird pantomime of make-believe authority practised on Delano.

The 'facts' seen by Delano are not facts at all, yet to the very last moment illusion persuaded him that it was reality. This is what Cereno sees, which entirely eludes Delano: a world where evil can impose itself unrecognised on innocence. In worldly terms Cereno is the failure. But perhaps, like Bartleby, he has seen more deeply into life than the practical Delano ever could.

How does Melville establish the atmosphere of doubt and deceit? By what means does he give the whole incident its wider, symbolic meaning? What, for example, in the final extract, is the significance of Cereno's scabbard? Do you feel that Cereno's appreciation of the events is more penetrating than Delano's? Generally, what is your response to the view of life expressed in these stories? Do you think Melville's method of presenting it effective? Do you sympathise with the two central characters?

'The Confidence-Man':
Melville as satirist

Style and meaning: intentional ambiguity

The Confidence-Man is a black, elliptical satire on America as Melville saw it—materialistic, avaricious, dishonest; hypocritically asserting trust and confidence, sanctimoniously paying homage to charity, credulous about moral and social progress—or exploiting that credulity.

The novel epitomises all this in a riverboat journey along the Mississippi on All Fools' Day. During it a confidence-man plies his trade, in a bewildering variety of disguises, among his fellow-passengers. It is more, however, than normal confidence-trickery, the novel more than a criticism of social iniquities. The confidence-man, constantly asserting his trust in human goodness, exposes the inadequacies, the fears, hatreds and hypocrisies of his gulls; the novel expresses the emptiness of a dissembling, mutable world where nothing can be taken at face value.

Among the *Fidèle*'s passengers is a crippled negro beggar. Accused of being an imposter, he describes several people on board who will speak for him. Most of these people appear as the novel develops. Gradually we realise that each of them is the confidence-man in a different guise; and that he has been the negro too.

In the first extract the confidence-man is John Ringman, 'the man with the weed' (crape, a sign of mourning, spurious here). He has just deceived a kindhearted merchant with a tale about his treatment by his heartless wife, Goneril, now dead. Now he is trying to soften up a student.

22

'Well, there is sorrow in the world, but goodness too; and goodness that is not greenness, either, no more than sorrow is. Dear good man. Poor beating heart!'

It was the man with the weed, not very long after quitting the merchant, murmuring to himself with his hand to his side like one with the heart-disease.

Meditation over kindness received seemed to have softened him something, too, it may be, beyond what might, perhaps, have been looked for from one whose unwonted self-respect in the hour of need, and in the act of being aided, might have appeared to some not wholly unlike pride out of place; and pride, in any place, is seldom very feeling. But the truth, perhaps, is, that those who are least touched with that vice, besides being not unsusceptible to goodness, are sometimes the ones whom a ruling sense of propriety makes appear cold, if not thankless, under a favor. For, at such a time, to be full of warm, earnest words, and heartfelt protestations, is to create a scene; and wellbred people dislike few things more than that; which would seem to look as if the world did not relish earnestness; but, not so; because the world, being earnest itself, likes an earnest scene, and an earnest man, very well, but only in their place—the stage. See what sad work they make of it, who, ignorant of this, flame out in Irish enthusiasm and with Irish sincerity, to a benefactor, who, if a man of sense and respectability, as well as kindliness, can but be more or less annoyed by it; and, if of a nervously fastidious nature, as some are, may be led to think almost as much less favorably of the beneficiary paining him by his gratitude, as if he had been guilty of its contrary, instead only of an indiscretion. But, beneficiaries who know better, though they may feel as much, if not more, neither inflict such pain, nor are inclined to run any risk of so doing. And these, being wise, are the majority. By which one sees how inconsiderate those persons are, who, from the absence of its officious manifestations in the world, complain that there is not much gratitude extant; when the truth is, that there is as much of it as there is of modesty; but, both being for the most part votarists of the shade, for the most part keep out of sight.

What started this was, to account, if necessary, for the changed air of the man with the weed, who, throwing off in private the cold garb of decorum, and so giving warmly loose to his genuine heart, seemed almost transformed into another being. This subdued air of softness, too, was toned with melancholy, melancholy unreserved; a thing which, however at variance with propriety, still the more attested his earnestness; for one knows not how it is, but it sometimes happens that, where earnestness is, there, also, is melancholy.

At the time, he was leaning over the rail at the boat's side, in his pensiveness, unmindful of another pensive figure near—a young gentleman with a swan-neck, wearing a lady-like open shirt collar, thrown back, and tied with a black ribbon. From a square, tableted broach, curiously engraved with Greek characters, he seemed a collegian—not improbably, a sophomore—on his travels; possibly, his first. A small book bound in Roman vellum was in his hand.

Overhearing his murmuring neighbor, the youth regarded him with some surprise, not to say interest. But, singularly for a collegian, being apparently of a retiring nature, he did not speak; when the other still more increased his diffidence by changing from soliloquy to colloquy, in a manner strangely mixed of familiarity and pathos.

The Confidence-Man, ch. 5

What do you gather from the second paragraph about Ringman's attitude when accepting the merchant's charity? How does his manner differ now? From such a difference one might suspect Ringman of adopting a pose. But Melville suggests a reason for the difference. What is this reason? Melville then ensures that this will not settle our doubts: simply by mentioning certain things, he makes us wonder about them. *Is* the man now 'giving warmly loose to his genuine heart'; is he really 'unmindful of another pensive figure near'; or is he indeed 'transformed into another being', adopting a new role for a new victim? Generally in Melville's later books, as in this extract, his object is to raise, not answer, questions; suggest possibilities, not declaim certainties. The chameleon-like confidence-man, and our problems in assessing him, are symptomatic of an uncertain, ambiguous world.

A little later and the confidence-man, whom the reader can now identify, appears as 'the man in gray', approaching another of his dupes, 'the stranger', declared to be both good and wealthy.

23

But, considering that goodness is no such rare thing among men—the world familiarly know the noun; a common one in every language—it was curious that what so signalized the stranger, and made him look like a kind of foreigner, among the crowd (as to some it may make him appear more or less unreal in this portraiture), was but the expression of so prevalent a quality. Such goodness seemed his, allied with such fortune, that, so far as his own personal experience could have gone, scarcely could he have known ill, physical or moral; and as for knowing or suspecting the latter in any serious degree (supposing such degree of it to be), by observation or philosophy; for that, probably, his nature, by its opposition, was imperfectly qualified, or from it wholly exempted. For the rest, he might have been five-and-fifty, perhaps sixty, but tall, rosy, between plump and portly, with a primy, palmy air, and for the time and place not to hint of his years, dressed with a strangely festive finish and elegance. The inner side of his coat-skirts was of white satin, which might have looked especially inappropriate, had it not seemed less a bit of mere tailoring than something of an emblem, as it were; an involuntary emblem, let us say, that what seemed so good about him was not all outside; no, the fine covering had a still finer lining. Upon one hand he wore a white kid glove, but the other hand, which was ungloved, looked hardly less white. Now, as the *Fidèle*, like most steamboats, was upon deck a little soot-streaked here and there, especially about the railings, it was a marvel how, under such circumstances, these hands retained their spotlessness. But, if you watched them a while, you noticed that they avoided touching anything; you noticed, in short, that a certain negro body-servant, whose hands nature had dyed black, perhaps with the same purpose that millers wear white, this negro servant's hands did most of his master's handling for him; having to do with dirt on his account, but not to his prejudice. But if, with the same undefiledness of consequences to himself, a gentleman could also sin by deputy, how shocking would that be! But it is not permitted to be; and even if it were, no judicious moralist would make proclamation of it.

This gentleman, therefore, there is reason to affirm, was one who, like the Hebrew governor,[1] knew how to keep his hands clean, and who never in his life happened to be run suddenly against by hurrying house-painter, or sweep; in a word, one whose very good luck it was to be a very good man.

Not that he looked as if he were a kind of Wilberforce[2] at all; that superior merit, probably, was not his; nothing

---

[1] i.e., Pontius Pilate.
[2] William Wilberforce (1759–1833); English statesman and humanitarian; a prime mover in the abolition of the slave traffic.

in his manner bespoke him righteous, but only good, and though to be good is much below being righteous, and though there is a difference between the two, yet not, it is to be hoped, so incompatible as that a righteous man can not be a good man; though, conversely, in the pulpit it has been with much cogency urged, that a merely good man, that is, one good merely by his nature, is so far from thereby being righteous, that nothing short of a total change and conversion can make him so; which is something which no honest mind, well read in the history of righteousness, will care to deny; nevertheless, since St. Paul himself, agreeing in a sense with the pulpit distinction, though not altogether in the pulpit deduction, and also pretty plainly intimating which of the two qualities in question enjoys his apostolic preference; I say, since St. Paul has so meaningly said, that, 'scarcely for a righteous man will one die, yet peradventure for a good man some would even dare to die;' therefore, when we repeat of this gentleman, that he was only a good man, whatever else by severe censors may be objected to him, it is still to be hoped that his goodness will not at least be considered criminal in him. At all events, no man, not even a righteous man, would think it quite right to commit this gentleman to prison for the crime, extraordinary as he might deem it; more especially, as, until everything could be known, there would be some chance that the gentleman might after all be quite as innocent of it as he himself.

It was pleasant to mark the good man's reception of the salute of the righteous man, that is, the man in gray; his inferior, apparently, not more in the social scale than in stature. Like the benign elm again, the good man seemed to wave the canopy of his goodness over that suitor, not in conceited condescension, but with that even amenity of true majesty, which can be kind to any one without stooping to it.

The Confidence-Man, ch. 7

Melville is not setting up the confidence-man (bad)

against his victims (good—or even pitiable). Most of the victims are either fools or frauds. Melville's purpose here, through his presentation of 'the stranger', is to question conventional ideas of goodness. He does this through a series of dazzling linguistic variations on what it signifies, '[a] flurry of phrases that modify, hesitantly contradict . . . leaving not a rack of positive statement behind.'[3]

Notice, for example, the ironic effect of repeating 'good' and 'goodness'. The stranger's goodness, too, seems to be based on inexperience and imperceptiveness. Melville does not put it like that—but which of his comments may we so interpret? The good man's use of gloves and the duty of his negro servant also imply his remoteness from life— he avoids 'having to do with dirt'. The last sentence of the third paragraph then adds that no one can secure 'undefiled- ness of consequence to himself' by using another to sin on his behalf. The second part of the sentence radically qualifies the statement by implying that there may be another view, adding a cynical comment about moralists. The casual comparison to Pontius Pilate further undermines the stranger's pretensions; and by the end his goodness has become a crime.

In passing, Melville has also made a distinction between goodness and righteousness and then queried their meaning —the 'pulpit distinction' between them seems to differ from that of St. Paul. Throughout, Melville is asking if anyone, however 'good' or 'righteous', can claim exemp- tion from the guilt common to man after the Fall. Do you find Melville's a satisfying method of raising these issues?

Stories as parables: the use of interpolated stories

Here the goodhearted merchant, Harry Roberts, re-appears.

[3] R. W. B. Lewis: Afterword to *The Confidence-Man*, Signet Classics, New York, 1964, p. 265.

Along with other incidents, Ringman's story about the morbidly cruel Goneril has profoundly depressed Roberts. Now he has met the confidence-man in yet another role—John Truman, coal company president—and has passed on to him the story of Goneril. Truman, who affects a jaunty confidence in the ways of the world and human nature, has set out to interpret Ringman's alleged experience more cheerfully: Goneril is dead, so all has worked out for the best.

24

But he thought he might be getting dry.[4]

The merchant, in his good-nature, thought otherwise, and said that he would be glad to refresh himself with such fruit all day. It was sitting under a ripe pulpit, and better such a seat than under a ripe peach-tree.

The other was pleased to find that he had not, as he feared, been prosing; but would rather not be considered in the formal light of a preacher; he preferred being still received in that of the equal and genial companion. To which end, throwing still more of sociability into his manner, he again reverted to the unfortunate man. Take the very worst view of that case; admit that his Goneril was, indeed, a Goneril; how fortunate to be at last rid of this Goneril, both by nature and by law? If he were acquainted with the unfortunate man, instead of condoling with him, he would congratulate him. Great good fortune had this unfortunate man. Lucky dog, he dared say, after all.

To which the merchant replied, that he earnestly hoped it might be so, and at any rate he tried his best to comfort himself with the persuasion that, if the unfortunate man was not happy in this world, he would, at least, be so in another.

His companion made no question of the unfortunate

---

[4] i.e., boring.

man's happiness in both worlds; and, presently calling for some champagne, invited the merchant to partake, upon the playful plea that, whatever notions other than felicitous ones he might associate with the unfortunate man, a little champagne would readily bubble away.

At intervals they slowly quaffed several glasses in silence and thoughtfulness. At last the merchant's expressive face flushed, his eye moistly beamed, his lips trembled with an imaginative and feminine sensibility. Without sending a single fume to his head, the wine seemed to shoot to his heart, and begin soothsaying there. 'Ah,' he cried, pushing his glass from him, 'Ah, wine is good, and confidence is good; but can wine or confidence percolate down through all the stony strata of hard considerations, and drop warmly and ruddily into the cold cave of truth? Truth will *not* be comforted. Led by dear charity, lured by sweet hope, fond fancy essays this feat; but in vain; mere dreams and ideals, they explode in your hand, leaving naught but the scorching behind!'

'Why, why, why!' in amaze, at the burst; 'bless me, if *In vino veritas* be a true saying, then, for all the fine confidence you professed with me, just now, distrust, deep distrust, underlies it; and ten thousand strong, like the Irish Rebellion, breaks out in you now. That wine, good wine, should do it! Upon my soul,' half seriously, half humorously, securing the bottle, 'you shall drink no more of it. Wine was meant to gladden the heart, not grieve it; to heighten confidence, not depress it.'

Sobered, shamed, all but confounded by this raillery, the most telling rebuke under such circumstances, the merchant stared about him, and then, with altered mien, stammeringly confessed, that he was almost as much surprised as his companion, at what had escaped him. He did not understand it; was quite at a loss to account for such a rhapsody popping out of him unbidden. It could hardly be the champagne; he felt his brain unaffected; in fact, if anything, the wine had acted upon it something like white of egg in coffee, clarifying and brightening.

'Brightening? brightening it may be, but less like the white of egg in coffee, than like stove-lustre on a stove—black, brightening seriously, I repent calling for the champagne. To a temperament like yours, champagne is not to be recommended. Pray, my dear sir, do you feel quite yourself again? Confidence restored?'

'I hope so; I think I may say it is so. But we have had a long talk, and I think I must retire now.'

So saying, the merchant rose, and making his adieus, left the table with the air of one, mortified at having been tempted by his own honest goodness, accidentally stimulated into making mad disclosures—to himself as to another —of the queer, unaccountable caprices of his natural heart.

The Confidence-Man, ch. 13

Roberts is one of the very few sympathetic characters in the novel. Significantly, even he is reluctant to abandon comforting illusions. This sequence is unusual in *The Confidence-Man* in allowing us to know what really is passing through a character's mind. The story of Goneril, though untrue, has in fact, for a time, opened the merchant's eyes —to what? By the end, Truman seems to have settled his doubts. What indications does Melville give us that his doubts are a more valuable experience than his restored confidence?

Frank Goodman—the confidence-man in his last role, as the 'cosmopolitan'—is talking to Charles Noble. Noble has been trying (unavailingly) to wear him down with drink with a view to trickery.

25

'In want of money!' pushing back his chair as from a suddenly-disclosed man-trap or crater.

'Yes,' naïvely assented the cosmopolitan, 'and you are

going to loan me fifty dollars. I could almost wish I was in need of more, only for your sake. Yes, my dear Charlie, for your sake; that you might the better prove your noble kindliness, my dear Charlie.'

'None of your dear Charlies,' cried the other, springing to his feet, and buttoning up his coat, as if hastily to depart upon a long journey.

'Why, why, why?' painfully looking up.

'None of your why, why, whys!' tossing out a foot, 'go to the devil, sir! Beggar, impostor!—never so deceived in a man in my life.'

The Confidence-Man, ch. 31

While speaking or rather hissing those words, the boon companion underwent much such a change as one reads of in fairy-books. Out of old materials sprang a new creature. Cadmus glided into the snake.

The cosmopolitan rose, the traces of previous feeling vanished; looked steadfastly at his transformed friend a moment, then, taking ten half-eagles[5] from his pocket, stooped down, and laid them, one by one, in a circle round him; and, retiring a pace, waved his long tasselled pipe with the air of a necromancer, an air heightened by his costume, accompanying each wave with a solemn murmur of cabalistical words.

Meantime, he within the magic ring stood suddenly rapt, exhibiting every symptom of a successful charm—a turned cheek, a fixed attitude, a frozen eye; spellbound, not more by the waving wand than by the ten invincible talismans on the floor.

'Reappear, reappear, reappear, oh, my former friend! Replace this hideous apparition with thy blest shape, and be the token of thy return the words, "My dear Frank."'

'My dear Frank,' now cried the restored friend, cordially stepping out of the ring, with regained self-possession regaining lost identity, 'My dear Frank, what a funny man you are; full of fun as an egg of meat. How could you tell

[5] eagle: a gold coin worth ten dollars.

me that absurd story of your being in need? But I relish a good joke too well to spoil it by letting on. Of course, I humored the thing; and, on my side, put on all the cruel airs you would have me. Come, this little episode of fictitious estrangement will but enhance the delightful reality. Let us sit down again, and finish our bottle.'

'With all my heart,' said the cosmopolitan, dropping the necromancer with the same facility with which he had assumed it. 'Yes,' he added, soberly picking up the gold pieces and returning them with a chink to his pocket, 'yes, I am something of a funny man now and then; while for you, Charlie,' eyeing him in tenderness, 'what you say about your humoring the thing is true enough; never did man second a joke better than you did just now. You played your part better than I did mine; you played it, Charlie, to the life.'

'You see, I once belonged to an amateur play company; that accounts for it. But come, fill up, and let's talk of something else.'

'Well,' acquiesced the cosmopolitan, seating himself, and quietly brimming his glass, 'what shall we talk about?'

'Oh, anything you please,' a sort of nervously accommodating.

'Well, suppose we talk about Charlemont?'

'Charlemont? What's Charlemont? Who's Charlemont?'

'You shall hear, my dear Charlie,' answered the cosmopolitan. 'I will tell you the story of Charlemont, the gentleman-madman.' . . .

The Confidence-Man, ch. 32

'Charlemont was a young merchant of French descent, living in St. Louis—a man not deficient in mind, and possessed of that sterling and captivating kindliness, seldom in perfection seen but in youthful bachelors, united at times to a remarkable sort of gracefully devil-may-care and witty good-humor. Of course, he was admired by everybody, and loved, as only mankind can love, by not a few. But in his twenty-ninth year a change came over him. Like one whose hair turns gray in a night, so in a day Charlemont turned from affable to morose. His acquaintances were passed without greeting; while, as for his confidential friends, them he pointedly, unscrupulously, and with a kind of fierceness, cut dead.

'One, provoked by such conduct, would fain have resented it with words as disdainful; while another, shocked by the change, and, in concern for a friend, magnanimously overlooking affronts, implored to know what sudden, secret grief had distempered him. But from resentment and from tenderness Charlemont alike turned away.

'Ere long, to the general surprise, the merchant Charlemont was gazetted, and the same day it was reported that he had withdrawn from town, but not before placing his entire property in the hands of responsible assignees for the benefit of creditors.

'Whither he had vanished, none could guess. At length, nothing being heard, it was surmised that he must have made away with himself—a surmise, doubtless, originating in the remembrance of the change some months previous to his bankruptcy—a change of a sort only to be ascribed to a mind suddenly thrown from its balance.

'Years passed. It was spring-time, and lo, one bright morning, Charlemont lounged into the St. Louis coffee-houses—gay, polite, humane, companionable, and dressed in the height of costly elegance. Not only was he alive, but he was himself again. Upon meeting with old acquaintances, he made the first advances, and in such a manner that it was impossible not to meet him half-way. Upon other old friends, whom he did not chance casually to meet, he either personally called, or left his card and compliments for them; and to several, sent presents of game or hampers of wine.

'They say the world is sometimes harshly unforgiving, but it was not so to Charlemont. The world feels a return of love for one who returns to it as he did. Expressive of its renewed interest was a whisper, an inquiring whisper, how now, exactly, so long after his bankruptcy, it fared with Charlemont's purse. Rumor, seldom at a loss for answers, replied that he had spent nine years in Marseilles in France, and there acquiring a second fortune, had returned with it, a man devoted henceforth to genial friendships.

'Added years went by, and the restored wanderer still the same; or rather, by his noble qualities, grew up like golden maize in the encouraging sun of good opinions. But still the latent wonder was, what had caused that change in him at a period when, pretty much as now, he was, to all appearance, in the possession of the same fortune, the same friends, the same popularity. But nobody thought it would be the thing to question him here.

'At last, at a dinner at his house, when all the guests but one had successively departed; this remaining guest, an old acquaintance, being just enough under the influence of wine to set aside the fear of touching upon a delicate point, ventured, in a way which perhaps spoke more favorably for his heart than his tact, to beg of his host to explain the one enigma of his life. Deep melancholy overspread the before cheery face of Charlemont; he sat for some moments tremulously silent; then pushing a full decanter towards the guest, in a choked voice, said: "No, no! when by art, and care, and time, flowers are made to bloom over a grave, who would seek to dig all up again only to know the mystery?—The wine." When both glasses were filled, Charlemont took his, and lifting it, added lowly: "If ever, in days to come, you shall see ruin at hand, and, thinking you understand mankind, shall tremble for your friendships, and tremble for your pride; and, partly through love for the one and fear for the other, shall resolve to be beforehand with the world, and save it from sin by prospectively taking that sin to yourself, then will you do as one I now dream of once did, and like him will you suffer; but how fortunate and how grateful should you be, if like him, after all that had happened, you could be a little happy again."

'When the guest went away, it was with the persuasion, that though outwardly restored in mind as in fortune, yet

some taint of Charlemont's old malady survived, and that
it was not well for friends to touch one dangerous string.'
The Confidence-Man, ch. 34

The story of Charlemont is a riddling one. Foreseeing
bankruptcy, he goes away, evidently afraid that the loss
of his money will lose him his friends. After the story,
Goodman insists that real life shows Charlemont's fears to
be illusory : no friend would turn against another suddenly
made penniless. Blandly, he affects not to recognise the
example of Noble's own conduct. But even his telling of
Charlemont's story hints otherwise : the world is not
'harshly unforgiving' to Charlemont—but forgives only
after it has satisfied itself about his finances. What are the
parallels between Goodman's experience with Noble and
Charlemont's history ? Is Charlemont's attitude the 'malady'
his confidant thinks it is ?

Charlemont's description of his 'prospectively taking' the
world's sin to himself, inevitably recalling the Crucifixion,
places Christ's selfless giving against Charlemont's dismal
assumption that friendship depends on money. Melville is
measuring human perversions of friendship, love, charity,
by the pure altruism of Christ. Do you find that this bears
upon Melville's earlier comments on 'goodness' and
'righteousness' ?

Still as Frank Goodman, the confidence-man has just had
a conversation with Mark Winsome, an idealist philosopher
(partly a satire on Emerson). His philosophy, Goodman de-
clares, is remote from the ideals of *practical* trust and
charity which the confidence-man unceasingly professes.
Winsome has left his disciple, Egbert, to continue the
debate.

The confidence-man proposes an elaborate make-believe
as the basis for their discussion : they are to talk as if they

were old friends, with Goodman asking Egbert for a loan. Egbert, furthermore, is to call himself Charlie—the confidence-man, obviously, is remembering his encounter with Charles Noble. Egbert-Charlie's first response to the request for money is to tell the story of China Aster, whom a friend has ruined by persuading him to accept loans which he does not need, and, in the end, cannot repay.

26

'With what heart,' cried Frank, still in character, 'have you told me this story? A story I can no way approve; for its moral, if accepted, would drain me of all reliance upon my last stay, and, therefore, of my last courage in life. For, what was that bright view of China Aster but a cheerful trust that, if he but kept up a brave heart, worked hard, and ever hoped for the best, all at last would go well? If your purpose, Charlie, in telling me this story, was to pain me, and keenly, you have succeeded; but, if it was to destroy my last confidence, I praise God you have not.'

'Confidence?' cried Charlie, who, on his side, seemed with his whole heart to enter into the spirit of the thing, 'what has confidence to do with the matter? That moral of the story, which I am for commending to you, is this: the folly, on both sides, of a friend's helping a friend. For was not that loan of Orchis to China Aster the first step towards their estrangement? And did it not bring about what in effect was the enmity of Orchis? I tell you, Frank, true friendship, like other precious things, is not rashly to be meddled with. And what more meddlesome between friends than a loan? A regular marplot. For how can you help that the helper must turn out a creditor? And creditor and friend, can they ever be one? no, not in the most lenient case; since, out of lenity to forgo one's claim, is less to be a friendly creditor than to cease to be a creditor at all. But it will not do to rely upon this lenity, no, not in the best man; for the best man, as the worst, is subject to all mortal contingencies. He may travel, he may marry, he may join the Come-Outers, or some equally untoward school or sect, not to speak of other things that more or less tend to new-cast the character. And were there nothing else, who shall answer for his digestion, upon which so much depends?'

'But Charlie, dear Charlie—'

'Nay, wait.—You have hearkened to my story in vain, if you do not see that, however indulgent and right-minded I may seem to you now, that is no guarantee for the future. And into the power of that uncertain personality which, through the mutability of my humanity, I may hereafter become, should not common sense dissuade you, my dear Frank, from putting yourself? Consider. Would you, in your present need, be willing to accept a loan from a friend, securing him by a mortgage on your homestead, and do so, knowing that you had no reason to feel satisfied that the mortgage might not eventually be transferred into the hands of a foe? Yet the difference between this man and that man is not so great as the difference between what the same man be to-day and what he may be in days to come. For there is no bent of heart or turn of thought which any man holds by virtue of an unalterable nature or will. Even those feelings and opinions deemed most identical with eternal right and truth, it is not impossible but that, as personal persuasions, they may in reality be but the result of some chance tip of Fate's elbow in throwing her dice. For, not to go into the first seeds of things, and passing by the accident of parentage predisposing to this or that habit of mind, descend below these, and tell me, if you change this man's experiences or that man's books, will wisdom go surety for his unchanged convictions? As particular food begets particular dreams, so particular experiences or books particular feelings or beliefs. I will hear nothing of that fine babble about development and its laws; there is no development in opinion and feeling but the developments of time and tide. You may deem all this

84

talk idle, Frank; but conscience bids me show you how fundamental the reasons for treating you as I do.'

'But Charlie, dear Charlie, what new notions are these? I thought that man was no poor drifting weed of the universe, as you phrased it; that, if so minded, he could have a will, a way, a thought, and a heart of his own? But now you have turned everything upside down again, with an inconsistency that amazes and shocks me.'

'Inconsistency? Bah!'

'There speaks the ventriloquist again,' sighed Frank, in bitterness.

Illy pleased, it may be, by this repetition of an allusion little flattering to his originality, however much so to his docility, the disciple sought to carry it off by exclaiming : 'Yes, I turn over day and night, with indefatigable pains, the sublime pages of my master, and unfortunately for you, my dear friend, I find nothing *there* that leads me to think otherwise than I do. But enough : in this matter the experience of China Aster teaches a moral more to the point than anything Mark Winsome can offer, or I either.'

'I cannot think so, Charlie; for neither am I China Aster, nor do I stand in his position. The loan to China Aster was to extend his business with; the loan I seek is to relieve my necessities.'

'Your dress, my dear Frank, is respectable; your cheek is not gaunt. Why talk of necessities when nakedness and starvation beget the only real necessities?'

'But I need relief, Charlie; and so sorely, that I now conjure you to forget that I was ever your friend, while I apply to you only as a fellow-being, whom, surely, you will not turn away.'

'That I will not. Take off your hat, bow over to the ground, and supplicate an alms of me in the way of London streets, and you shall not be a sturdy beggar in vain. But no man drops pennies into the hat of a friend, let me tell you. If you turn beggar, then, for the honor of noble friendship, I turn stranger.'

'Enough,' cried the other, rising, and with a toss of his

shoulders seeming disdainfully to throw off the character he had assumed. 'Enough. I have had my fill of the philosophy of Mark Winsome as put into action. And moonshiny as it in theory may be, yet a very practical philosophy it turns out in effect, as he himself engaged I should find. But, miserable for my race should I be, if I thought he spoke truth when he claimed, for proof of the soundness of his system, that the study of it tended to much the same formation of character with the experiences of the world. —Apt disciple! Why wrinkle the brow, and waste the oil both of life and the lamp, only to turn out a head kept cool by the under ice of the heart? What your illustrious magian has taught you, any poor, old, broken-down, heartshrunken dandy might have lisped. Pray, leave me, and with you take the last dregs of your inhuman philosophy, And here, take this shilling, and at the first wood-landing buy yourself a few chips to warm the frozen natures of you and your philosopher by.'

With these words and a grand scorn the cosmopolitan turned on his heel, leaving his companion at a loss to determine where exactly the fictitious character had been dropped, and the real one, if any, resumed. If any, because, with pointed meaning, there occurred to him, as he gazed after the cosmopolitan, these familiar lines:

> 'All the world's a stage,
> And all the men and women merely players,
> Who have their exits and their entrances,
> And one man in his time plays many parts.'
>
> *The Confidence-Man*, ch. 41

Goodman's encounters with Noble and Egbert, the stories of Charlemont and China Aster all expose the hollow friendships of a commercial society where money corrupts human relationships and, even worse, reduces the exalted concept of Charity (i.e. Christian love) to almsgiving.

This particular conversation, however, poses questions perhaps even more disturbing. It draws us into a masquerade of assumed personalities and mirror-images of past events: where, in all these mutations, is the real human being? on what, in a world so full of dissimulation, can we depend? can we be certain even of our own identity? How does the situation set up here by the confidence-man reflect such a world? How are Egbert's speculations about human nature appropriate to a world like that? Not even the hardheaded Egbert, though, controls events: he is another of the confidence-man's puppets.

The Confidence-Man is a bleak but not a despairing book. Melville has complete intellectual control of ideas and feelings. The prose, so different from *Moby Dick*'s exuberance, is icy, cerebral, precise; the incidents establish a pattern of cross-bearings as facet after facet of their meaning turns into view. The novel lacks 'action'; it has the drama and tension of ideas, attitudes, personalities, in conflict.

It is Melville's most 'impersonal' novel. Nowhere else does he so consistently withdraw from any direct expression of final judgment, leaving the reader to absorb his multiplying ambiguities. In this it certainly speaks for Melville's own troubled disillusionment with the slap-happy optimism of his society; and marks a crucial phase in his appraisal of Christian doctrine. Yet the satire has its positive values. Melville's commitment is to the creative strength of Christian love, its presence fleetingly declared even in this record of its betrayal. It is the function of the confidence-man to open our eyes to the nature and extent of this betrayal. As a critic has said, he 'is not the bringer of darkness; he is the one who reveals the darkness in ourselves.' Here, Melville explores that darkness.

'Billy Budd':
final views and their expression

With the failure of *The Confidence-Man* Melville ceased to seek publication. Established in his Customs House post, he turned to the writing of poetry. Perhaps his successive failures with the public set him against writing novels; perhaps his restless urge to experiment; the reasons are lost to us. At the end, however, he returned to prose fiction with *Billy Budd*.

Factually, it is based on the English Naval mutinies at Spithead, and on a mutiny on the U.S. Navy brig *Somers*, which involved a cousin of Melville's. Again it is a simple story. Aboard the English ship *Indomitable* Billy Budd, the innocent, the Handsome Sailor, arouses the antagonism of the satanic master-at-arms, Claggart. Before the captain, Vere, Claggart accuses Billy of planning mutiny. Billy strikes and kills him and, in the dangerous times of the French Revolutionary war, is hanged as an example to the Fleet. He submits willingly to his death. Legality and expediency have defeated charity and mercy.

The psychology of good and evil

The first extract analyses Claggart's psychology, and his antipathy to Billy.

In a list of definitions included in the authentic translation of Plato, a list attributed to him, occurs this: 'Natural Depravity: a depravity according to nature.' A definition which, though savoring of Calvinism, by no means involves Calvin's[1] dogma as to total mankind. Evidently its intent makes it applicable but to individuals. Not many are the examples of this depravity which the gallows and jail supply. At any rate, for notable instances, since these have no vulgar alloy of the brute in them, but invariably are dominated by intellectuality, one must go elsewhere. Civilization, especially if of the austerer sort, is auspicious to it. It folds itself in the mantle of respectability. It has its certain negative virtues serving as silent auxiliaries. It never allows wine to get within its guard. It is not going too far to say that it is without vices or small sins. There is a phenomenal pride in it that excludes them from anything mercenary or avaricious. In short the depravity here meant partakes nothing of the sordid or sensual. It is serious, but free from acerbity. Though no flatterer of mankind it never speaks ill of it.

But the thing which in eminent instances signalizes so exceptional a nature is this: though the man's even temper and discreet bearing would seem to intimate a mind peculiarly subject to the law of reason, not the less in his heart he would seem to riot in complete exemption from that law, having apparently little to do with reason further than to employ it as an ambidexter implement for effecting the irrational. That is to say: toward the accomplishment of an aim which in wantonness of malignity would seem to partake of the insane, he will direct a cool judgment sagacious and sound.

These men are true madmen, and of the most dangerous sort, for their lunacy is not continuous but occasional, evoked by some special object; it is probably secretive,

[1] John Calvin (1509–64): the theologian whose ideas shaped the doctrines of the Presbyterian Church.

which is as much to say it is self-contained, so that when, moreover, most active, it is to the average mind not distinguishable from sanity, and for the reason above suggested, that, whatever its aims may be—and the aim is never declared—the method and the outward proceeding are always perfectly rational.

Now something such was Claggart, in whom was the mania of an evil nature, not engendered by vicious training or corrupting books or licentious living but born with him and innate, in short 'a depravity according to nature'. . . .

Billy Budd, ch. 11

That Claggart's figure was not amiss, and his face, save the chin, well molded, has already been said. Of these favorable points he seemed not insensible, for he was not only neat but careful in his dress. But the form of Billy Budd was heroic; and if his face was without the intellectual look of the pallid Claggart's not the less was it lit, like his, from within, though from a different source. The bonfire in his heart made luminous the rose-tan in his cheek.

In view of the marked contrast between the persons of the twain, it is more than probable that when the master-at-arms in the scene last given applied to the sailor the proverb *Handsome is as handsome does* he let there escape an ironic inkling, not caught by the young sailors who heard it, as to what it was that had first moved him against Billy, namely, his significant personal beauty.

Now envy and antipathy, passions irreconcilable in reason, nevertheless in fact may spring conjoined like Chang and Eng[2] in one birth. Is Envy then such a monster? Well, though many an arraigned mortal has in hopes of mitigated penalty pleaded guilty to horrible actions, did ever anybody seriously confess to envy? Something there is in it universally felt to be more shameful than even felonious crime. And not only does everybody disown it

[2] A famous pair of Siamese twins (1811–74).

but the better sort are inclined to incredulity when it is in earnest imputed to an intelligent man. But since its lodgment is in the heart, not the brain, no degree of intellect supplies a guarantee against it. But Claggart's was no vulgar form of the passion. Nor, as directed toward Billy Budd, did it partake of that streak of apprehensive jealousy which marred Saul's visage, perturbedly brooding on the comely young David. Claggart's envy struck deeper. If askance he eyed the good looks, cheery health, and frank enjoyment of young life in Billy Budd, it was because these went along with a nature that, as Claggart magnetically felt, had in its simplicity never willed malice or experienced the reactionary bite of that serpent. To him, the spirit lodged within Billy and looking out from his welkin eyes as from windows, that ineffability it was which made the dimple in his dyed cheek, suppled his joints, and, dancing in his yellow curls, made him preëminently the Handsome Sailor. One person excepted, the master-at-arms was perhaps the only man in the ship intellectually capable of adequately appreciating the moral phenomenon presented in Billy Budd. And the insight but intensified his passion, which, assuming various secret forms within him, at times assumed that of cynic disdain—disdain of innocence—to be nothing more than innocent! Yet in an aesthetic way he saw the charm of it, the courageous free-and-easy temper of it, and fain would have shared it, but he despaired of it.

With no power to annul the elemental evil in him, though readily enough he could hide it; apprehending the good, but powerless to be it; a nature like Claggart's surcharged with energy as such natures almost invariably are, what recourse is left to it but to recoil upon itself, and, like the scorpion for which the Creator alone is responsible, act out to the end the part allotted it.

Billy Budd, ch. 13

Claggart is Melville's final treatment of a recurrent type in his novels—Jackson, Babo, Bland in *White-Jacket*, Radney in 'The *Town-Ho's* Story' in *Moby Dick*. Competent, often withdrawn, elegant, even effeminate, their nature is inherently evil, no more able to resist its destructive impulses than to cease breathing. They are the human embodiment of all the baneful elements on earth. Where does Melville suggest this wider significance in Claggart?

Here, the sober, austere prose itemises Claggart's involuted nature. What paradoxes in it does Melville isolate? Claggart hates Billy because in him he recognises his opposite. Billy in fact is not perfect. A stammer prevents his answering Claggart's accusation so that, thus impotent, he strikes Claggart, bringing about his own undoing. Also, his innocence has no awareness—a 'moral phenomenon' it is called. So Claggart's is not ordinary envy. With it he feels his own superior merit. Why does he feel this superiority? Is it purely on grounds of intellect—which we gather Billy lacks? Or is Billy's very innocence in some way a deficiency?

Moral by implication

At the end of *Billy Budd* Melville sets together three sequels to the main action.

28

The symmetry of form attainable in pure fiction cannot so readily be achieved in a narration essentially having less to do with fable than with fact. Truth uncompromisingly told will always have its ragged edges; hence the conclusion of such a narration is apt to be less finished than an architectural finial.

How it fared with the Handsome Sailor during the year of the great mutiny has been faithfully given. But though properly the story ends with his life, something in way of sequel will not be amiss. Three brief chapters will suffice.

In the general re-christening under the Directory of the craft originally forming the navy of the French Monarchy, the *St. Louis* line-of-battle ship was named the *Athéiste*. Such a name, like some other substituted ones in the Revolutionary fleet, while proclaiming the infidel audacity of the ruling power was yet, though not so intended to be, the aptest name, if one consider it, ever given to a warship; far more so indeed than the *Devastation*, the *Erebus* (the *Hell*) and similar names bestowed upon fighting ships.

On the return passage to the English fleet from the detached cruise during which occurred the events already recorded, the *Indomitable* fell in with the *Athéiste*. An engagement ensued, during which Captain Vere, in the act of putting his ship alongside the enemy with a view of throwing his boarders across the bulwarks, was hit by a musket-ball from a port-hole of the enemy's main cabin. More than disabled he dropped to the deck and was carried below to the same cock-pit where some of his men already lay. The senior lieutenant took command. Under him the enemy was finally captured and though much crippled was by rare good fortune successfully taken into Gibraltar, an English port not very distant from the scene of the fight. There Captain Vere with the rest of the wounded was put ashore. He lingered for some days, but the end came. Unhappily he was cut off too early for the Nile and Trafalgar. The spirit that spite its philosophic austerity may yet have indulged in the most secret of all passions, ambition, never attained to the fullness of fame.

Not long before death, while lying under the influence of that magical drug which, soothing the physical frame, mysteriously operates on the subtler element in man, he was heard to murmur words inexplicable to his attendant —'Billy Budd, Billy Budd.' That these were not the accents of remorse, would seem clear from what the attendant said to the *Indomitable*'s senior officer of marines, who, as the most reluctant to condemn of the members of the drum-

head court, too well knew, though here he kept the knowledge to himself, who Billy Budd was.

Billy Budd, ch. 29

Some few weeks after the execution, among other matters
under the head of *News from the Mediterranean*, there
appeared in a naval chronicle of the time, an authorized
weekly publication, an account of the affair. It was doubtless for the most part written in good faith, though the
medium, partly rumor, through which the facts must have
reached the writer, served to deflect and in part falsify
them. The account was as follows:—

'On the tenth of the last month a deplorable occurrence
took place on board H.M.S. *Indomitable*. John Claggart, the
ship's master-at-arms, discovering that some sort of plot
was incipient among an inferior section of the ship's company, and that the ringleader was one William Budd, he,
Claggart, in the act of arraigning the man before the Captain was vindictively stabbed to the heart by the suddenly
drawn sheath-knife of Budd.

'The deed and the implement employed sufficiently suggest that, though mustered into the service under an English
name, the assassin was no Englishman, but one of those
aliens adopting English cognomens whom the present extraordinary necessities of the Service have caused to be
admitted into it in considerable numbers.

'The enormity of the crime and the extreme depravity of
the criminal, appear the greater in view of the character
of the victim, a middle-aged man respectable and discreet,
belonging to that minor official grade, the petty-officers,
upon whom, as none know better than the commissioned
gentlemen, the efficiency of His Majesty's navy so largely
depends. His function was a responsible one, at once onerous
and thankless, and his fidelity in it the greater because of
his strong patriotic impulse. In this instance, as in so many
other instances in these days, the character of this unfortunate man signally refutes, if refutation were needed,
that peevish saying attributed to the late Dr. Johnson, that
patriotism is the last refuge of a scoundrel.

'The criminal paid the penalty of his crime. The promptitude of the punishment has proved salutary. Nothing amiss is now apprehended aboard H.M.S. *Indomitable*.'

The above, appearing in a publication now long ago superannuated and forgotten, is all that hitherto has stood in human record to attest what manner of men respectively were John Claggart and Billy Budd.

Billy Budd, ch. 30

Everything is for a term remarkable in navies. Any tangible object associated with some striking incident of the service is converted into a monument. The spar from which the foretopman was suspended was for some few years kept trace of by the bluejackets. Their knowledge followed it from ship to dockyard and again from dockyard to ship, still pursuing it even when at last reduced to a mere dockyard boom. To them a chip of it was as a piece of the Cross. Ignorant though they were of the secret facts of the tragedy, and not thinking but that the penalty was somehow unavoidably inflicted from the naval point of view, for all that they instinctively felt that Billy was a sort of man as incapable of mutiny as of willful murder. They recalled the fresh young image of the Handsome Sailor, that face never deformed by a sneer or subtler vile freak of the heart within! This impression of him was doubtless deepened by the fact that he was gone, and in a measure mysteriously gone. At the time on the gun-decks of the *Indomitable*, the general estimate of his nature and its unconscious simplicity eventually found rude utterance from another foretopman, one of his own watch, gifted, as some sailors are, with an artless poetic temperament; the tarry hands made some lines which, after circulating among the shipboard crew for a while, finally got rudely printed at Portsmouth as a ballad. The title given to it was the sailor's.[3]

Billy Budd, ch. 31

The naval chronicle draws a plain, direct moral from its

[3] The concluding poem, 'Billy in the Darbies' is omitted here.

story: right (Claggart) and wrong (Billy) have clashed; right has been avenged; discipline restored; victory ensured. We see immediately that the reporting is inaccurate—Claggart is not 'right'. It is true that the *Indomitable* has won a victory—but not because an exemplary execution has subdued a mutinous crew. The other sequels delicately correct this crude misinterpretation of Billy's death and his willing submission to it.

Billy's tragedy re-enacts the Crucifixion: the processes of law destroy innocence, which bows to its fate; and a chip from Billy's gallows becomes 'as a piece of the Cross'. This does not mean that Billy is Christ. But he has something of the same pure goodness, which lives beyond apparent defeat in the hearts of his companions, who also see 'that the penalty was somehow unavoidably inflicted'. Discreetly, Melville is suggesting a reading of the events different from the naval chronicle's both in meaning and in kind. The chronicle reduces a complex interplay of good and evil to crude melodrama.

How and where do the first and third of these chapters correct the impression given by the second? What is your interpretation of the story?

Billy Budd expresses a mood at least resigned, perhaps reconciled, to the ways of God to man. Billy's death generates a new stirring of the spirit and for all its tragic irony is not wholly wasted. The mood is tranquil. Yet in Melville's world good is still vulnerable to evil, and spiritual perfection alien. He offers no complacent solace. Loss and suffering are part of life. Good and evil appear in ambiguous, disturbing forms; simplicity may be a readier ally of evil than of good. Yet from their conflict some testimony to the power of good may obscurely survive.

Bibliography

Works by Melville

(Only Melville's major writings, are listed. A. R. Humphreys, *Melville*—see page 99—has a useful bibliography).

Typee, London and New York, 1846. Also: (i) World's Classics, London (Oxford University Press), 1924; (ii) ed. Milton R. Stern, Everyman's Library (with *Billy Budd*), London (Dent) and New York (Dutton), 1958; (iii) Anchor Books, New York (Doubleday), 1957.

Omoo, New York and London, 1847. Also: (i) World's Classics, London, 1924; (ii) Evergreen Books, New York (Grove Press) and London (Calder), 1958.

Mardi, London and New York, 1849. Also: Signet Classics, New York (New American Library), 1964.

Redburn, New York and London, 1849. Also: Anchor Books, New York, 1957.

White-Jacket, New York and London, 1850. Also: (i) ed. Carl Van Doren, World's Classics, London, 1924; (ii) ed. William Plomer, Chiltern Library, London (John Lehmann), 1952; (iii) Evergreen Books, New York and London, 1956; (iv) ed. A. R. Humphreys, Classic American Texts, London (Oxford University Press), 1966.

Moby Dick, London and New York, 1851. Also: (i) with an introduction by J. N. Sullivan, London (Collins), 1953; (ii) ed. Sherman Paul, Everyman's Library, London, 1954; (iii) ed. H. Beaver, World's Classics, London, 1959; (iv) with an Afterword by Denham Sutcliffe, Signet Classics, New York, 1961.

Pierre, New York, 1852. Also: with a Foreword by Lawrance Thompson, Signet Classics, New York, 1964

Israel Potter, New York, 1854.

The Piazza Tales, New York, 1856. Also: Anchor Books (with *Billy Budd*), New York (n.d.).

The Confidence-Man, New York, 1857. Also: (i) ed. Roy Fuller, Chiltern Library, London, 1948; (ii) Evergreen Books, New York and London, 1955; (iii) with an Afterword by R. W. B. Lewis, Signet Classics, New York, 1964.

Battle-Pieces and Aspects of War (Poems), New York, 1866.

Clarel (A Poem), New York, 1876.

Billy Budd, Written c.1888; first pub. 1924. F. Barron Freeman ed. (corrected Elizabeth Treeman), is the definitive text. Also: (i) in R. Chase ed. *Herman Melville Selected Tales and Poems* (with *Benito Cereno*, *Bartleby* and other tales and poems), Holt, Rinehart & Winston, New York, 1951; (ii) ed. Rex Warner, Chiltern Library, London, 1951; (iii) in *Herman Melville Four Short Novels* (with *Benito Cereno*, *Bartleby*, *The Encantadas*) Bantam Classics, New York, 1959; (iv) with an Afterword by Willard Thorp, *Billy Budd and other Tales* (with *Benito Cereno*, *Bartleby* and other tales) Signet Classics, New York, 1961; (v) in J. Leyda ed. *The Portable Melville*, The Viking Press, New York, 1952. See also under *Typee* and *The Piazza Tales*.

The Letters of Herman Melville, ed. Merril R. Davies and William H. Gilman, Yale University Press, New Haven, 1960.

Collected Poems, ed. Howard P. Vincent, Packard & Co.,

Hendricks House, Chicago, 1947; also *Selected Poems,*
ed. Hennig Cohen, Doubleday Anchor, New York, 1964.
Journal of a Visit to London and the Continent, 1849–1850,
ed. E. M. Metcalf, Cohen & West, London, 1949.
Journal of a Visit to Europe and the Levant, 1856–1857, ed.
Howard C. Horsford, Princeton University Press, Princeton, 1955.

Books wholly devoted to Melville

ARVIN, NEWTON, *Herman Melville,* University of California
Press, Berkeley and Los Angeles, 1951; Methuen, London,
1951. A critical biography; at its best in criticism on
the major novels, less responsive to some of the later
books, generally the most discriminating combination
of 'life' and 'works'.

CHASE, RICHARD, *Herman Melville: A Critical Study,* Mac-
millan, New York, 1949. Examines particularly Melville's
use of myth and folklore in the design of the novels,
sometimes a little fine-spun in its speculations, but full
of illuminating ideas.

CHASE, RICHARD, ed., *Herman Melville: A Collection of
Critical Essays,* Prentice Hall, New Jersey, 1962. Essays
by various critics on most aspects of Melville. Gives
generous consideration to the 'early' and 'later' novels.

GILMAN, WILLIAM, *Melville's Early Life and 'Redburn',* Oxford University Press, London, 1951; New York University Press, New York, 1951. A thorough account of
Melville's youth, showing exactly what use he made of
his experiences in *Redburn,* and how fact and fiction
differ.

HOWARD, LEON, *Herman Melville,* University of California
Press, Berkeley, 1951. A biography giving a very complete factual account of Melville's life.

HUMPHREYS, A. R., *Melville,* Oliver & Boyd, Edinburgh and

London, 1962. A brief introductory study giving a very clear outline of Melville's life and works, with illuminating short commentaries on individual works.

LEYDA, JAY, *The Melville Log: A Documentary of Herman Melville* (2 vols.), Harcourt Brace, New York, 1929. A fascinating chronological collection of photographs, reviews, letters, documents of all sorts from Melville's life; not all of equal importance, but giving very substantial background.

MASON, RONALD, *The Spirit Above the Dust*, John Lehmann, London, 1951. Largely straight interpretative criticism, not laying stress on Melville's life. Useful chapters on *Pierre* and *Moby Dick*.

MAYOUX, JEAN-JACQUES, *Melville*, Evergreen Books, London, 1960; Grove Press, New York, 1960. Another good short introduction, very clear on Melville's symbolism and on the American background, and with interesting illustrations.

MUMFORD, LEWIS, *Herman Melville*, Harcourt Brace, New York, 1929. An early 'life' in some ways outmoded by more recent scholarship, and a bit over-dramatised in presentation, but still an understanding appreciation of the man.

OLSON, CHARLES, *Call me Ishmael*, London, Evergreen Books, 1958; New York, Grove Press, 1958. Interesting on some of Melville's literary affiliations.

SEDGWICK, W. E., *Herman Melville: The Tragedy of Mind*, Harvard University Press, Cambridge, Mass., 1944. One of the best critical studies, though silent on 'Benito Cereno'; a sensitive interpretation of Melville's ideas as they appear in his novels.

Books in part devoted to Melville

BEWLEY, MARIUS, *The Eccentric Design. Form in the Classic*

American Novel. Chatto and Windus, London, 1959. Examines the response of the major American novelists to the conflicting political philosophies of their times; the Melville chapter centres on *Moby Dick*.

LEWIS, R. W. B., *The American Adam. Innocence, Tragedy and Tradition in the Nineteenth Century*, University of Chicago Press, Chicago, 1955. The ideal of 'innocence' in the American experience as it shaped the thinking of American novelists; traces the theme in Melville through *Redburn*, *Moby Dick* and *Billy Budd*.

MATTHIESSEN, F. O., *The American Rennaissance*, Oxford University Press, London and New York, 1941. A brilliant critical account of the literature of late nineteenth-century America; the best short analysis of Melville in relation to his contemporaries and his times.

MAXWELL, D. E. S., *American Fiction. The Intellectual Background*, Routledge and Kegan Paul, London, 1963; Columbia University Press, New York, 1963. A general survey of American novelists from Cooper to the present, with a chapter placing Melville and Hawthorne primarily in the 'conservative' tradition of American thought.